THE MEMORIZED TORAH

Program in Judaic Studies
Brown University
BROWN JUDAIC STUDIES
Edited by
Jacob Neusner,
Wendell S. Dietrich, Ernest S. Frerichs,
Calvin Goldscheider, Alan Zuckerman

Project Editors (Project)

David Blumenthal, Emory University (Approaches to Medieval Judaism)
William Brinner (Studies in Judaism and Islam)
Ernest S. Frerichs, Brown University (Dissertations and Monographs)
Lenn Evan Goodman, University of Hawaii (Studies in Medieval Judaism) (Studies in
Judaism and Islam)
William Scott Green, University of Rochester (Approaches to Ancient Judaism)
Ivan Marcus, Jewish Theological Seminary of America
(Texts and Studies in Medieval Judaism)
Marc L. Raphael, Ohio State University (Approaches to Judaism in Modern Times)
Norbert Samuelson, Temple University (Jewish Philosophy)
Jonathan Z. Smith, University of Chicago (Studia Philonica)

Number 96
THE MEMORIZED TORAH
The Mnemonic System of the Mishnah
by
Jacob Neusner

THE MEMORIZED TORAH
The Mnemonic System of the Mishnah

by
Jacob Neusner

Scholars Press
Chico, California

BM
497.8
.N477
1985

THE MEMORIZED TORAH
The Mnemonic System of the Torah

by
Jacob Neusner

Library of Congress Cataloging in Publication Data

Neusner, Jacob, 1932-
   The memorized Torah.

   (Brown Judaic studies ; 96)
   Bibliography: p.
   Includes index.
   1. Mishnah—Mnemonic devices. I. Title. II. Series: Brown
Judaic studies ; no. 96.
BM497.8.N477 1985   296.1'2306   85-2450
ISBN 0-89130-866-0 (alk. paper)
ISBN 0-89130-867-9 (pbk. : alk. paper)

Printed in the United States of America
on acid-free paper

For

Rabbi Alan Yuter

Who serves a synagogue in the way a rabbi should, as a person of conviction and conscience,

and who, maintaining that good theology cannot come from bad scholarship, proves his point by producing out of authentic learning an important message of Judaism.

May there be many like him in Israel.

CONTENTS

CONTENTS (continued)

PREFACE

Judaism maintains that when Moses received the Torah from God at Mount Sinai, it came to him in two media. One was the Torah in writing. The other was the Torah "shebe^{C}al peh," ordinarily translated as "oral Torah." But the Hebrew words mean "that which is memorized," hence, "the memorized Torah." This book deals with the Mishnah, which is the first document of that part of the Torah that in Judaic myth came to Israel in the medium of memory, "the memorized Torah." Here I ask about memorizing the memorized Torah, that is to say, the mnemonic system revealed through the medium of oral formulation and oral transmission by means of memorization. Specifically, if, as I maintain along with all students of the Mishnah, the Mishnah is a book formulated and transmitted by means of memorization, exactly how does the formulation of the document facilitate remembering its exact words?

The Mishnah, a law code based on philosophical principles current in its age, ca. A.D. 200, frames its ideas in syllogistic patterns. The smallest whole units of discourse (cognitive units), defined as groups of sentences that make a point completely and entirely on their own, become intelligible on three bases: logical, topical, and rhetorical. What I prove in this book is simple: It is the confluence of logic, topic, and rhetoric that generates at the deepest structure of the Mishnah's language a set of mnemonic patterns. These mnemonics serve by definition to facilitate the easy memorization of the text of the Mishnah.

As I explain in the introduction, the Mishnah is divided into tractates, each defined by a given subject. The tractates are subdivided into what I call intermediate units of tradition ("chapters"), and the intermediate units are comprised of the smallest whole units of discourse or cognitive units.

What marks the smallest whole unit of discourse -- a handful of sentences? It is that the several sentences of which it is composed are unintelligible or not wholly intelligible by themselves but are entirely intelligible when seen as a group.

The smallest whole unit of discourse in the Mishnah invariably constitutes a syllogism, that is, a statement of a proposition, in which a condition or question, constituting a protasis, finds resolution in a rule or answer, the apodosis: If such and such is the case, then so and so is the rule -- that is the characteristic cognitive structure of the Mishnah's smallest whole unit of thought or discourse. Even if that statement were made up of two or three or even five declarative sentences, it is only when the proposition is fully exposed, both protasis and apodosis, that the declarative sentences reach the level of full and complete expression, that is, sense and intelligibility.

In this book I show the principles by which the apodosis and protasis of the Mishnah's smallest whole units of discourse are framed in formal, mnemonic patterns. The patterns of language, e.g., syntactic structures, follow a few simple rules. These rules, once

- 1 -

known, apply nearly everywhere. They permit anyone to reconstruct, out of a few key-phrases, an entire cognitive unit, and, more important, as we shall see, complete intermediate units of discourse.

Let me unpack this critical claim. An intermediate unit of discourse serves to make a single point, that is, to present a given logical proposition. The logical proposition (for example, a general or encompassing rule) rarely comes to articulate expression. Rather, it will be given a set of concrete exemplifications. Three or five or more cases will make the point in detail. Put together, they turn out to express, through examples, a logical proposition. That is what I mean in referring to logic and topic. The underlying logic ordinarily is expressed only in topical form, through concrete instances of what only seldom is stated in so many words.

What is the place of rhetoric? What I have proven in earlier work and will spell out here is a simple fact. A single rhetorical pattern will govern the whole set of topical instances of a logical proposition. When the logical-topical program changes, the rhetorical pattern will change too. So, as I said, the mnemonics of the Mishnah rest on the confluence of (1) deep logic, (2) articulated topic, and (3) manifest rhetoric. Working downward from the surface, anyone can penetrate into the deeper layers of meaning of the Mishnah. Then and at the same time, while discovering the principle behind the cases, one can easily memorize the whole by mastering the recurrent rhetorical pattern dictating the expression of the cogent set of cases. For it is easy to note the shift from one rhetorical pattern to another and to follow the repeated cases, articulated in the new pattern downward to its logical substrate.

So syllogistic propositions, in the Mishnah's authors' hands, come to full expression not only in what people wish to state but also in how they choose to say it. The limits of rhetoric define the arena of topical articulation. Once we ask what three or five joined topical propositions have in common, we state the logic shared among them all.

In discourse such as this, aesthetics, of which mnemonics constitutes a subdivision, joins to topic and logic in the expression of philosophy. True, the gifted author, Plato, as represented in The Dialogues, finds guidance in an aesthetics more immediately accessible than the one at hand. At issue in what Socrates and Plato say, likewise, are matters anyone can find important, even urgent. And yet the arcane and tedious detail of the Mishnah too comprises a set of statements on a program of philosophy and metaphysics, ethics and politics. That program proves no less philosophical, no less pertinent to the life of the people, than the Dialogues, on the one side, and the Republic, on the other. In the age of the Second Sophistic the backcountry philosophers of Galilee in the later second century worried about being and becoming, the potential and the actual, the nature of mixtures, the good life, and the ideal state. Their program of reflection will not have surprised the metropolitan figures, the street-corner preachers with their sizable followings, the philosophers of note and fame. True, the raw materials sages used for the expression of their program will have astounded their contemporaries, in the Second Sophistic, if, to begin with, they had known the topical program at hand. But the sole difference between Stoic physicists, the philosophers who spoke about mixtures, and the

Mishnah's physicists, the philosophers who spoke about rennet and cheese, gravy, mixed seeds, and linen and wool, lies not in logic but in topic and, obviously, in rhetoric.

In addressing such matters, I have moved far beyond the program of this book. What I propose to accomplish here is simply the statement of certain mnemonic principles I have discovered, together with a complete repertoire of references to the texts in which I discovered them. In fact everything here has been in print for well over a decade. I have found, however, that one of the two books, a small part of which I represent here, never had a single review. The few reviewers of the other never dealt with the subject of mnemonics. My hope is that by putting together what I have found about the topic, I may gain that hearing that until now has not been accorded to what I believe are matters of some interest and value. The never-reviewed book is my History of the Mishnaic Law of Purities (Leiden, 1977). XXI. The Redaction and Formulation of the Order of Purities in the Mishnah and Tosefta. The other is my Rabbinic Traditions about the Pharisees before 70 (Leiden, 1971) III. Conclusions. The former deals with the protasis of the smallest whole unit of discourse in the Mishnah, the latter with the apodosis. Since the principles of the formation of the apodosis, in the material surveyed, prove rather simple, I deal with them first, and turn, in Chapters Two and Three, to the protasis.

INTRODUCTION

The Mishnah, a philosophical law-code that reached closure at ca. A.D. 200, is divided into tractates, chapters, and paragraphs. We know when a tractate begins and ends because tractates are organized by subject-matter. "Chapters" by contrast constitute conventions of printers. There is little internal evidence that the framers of the document broke up the tractates along the lines followed by the copyists and printers of medieval and early modern times. What we have within tractates are subunits on problems or themes presented by the basic topic of the tractate. These subunits or themes are characterized by the confluence of formal and substantive traits. That is to say, a given formal pattern characterizes discourse on a given substantive problem. When the topic or problem changes, the formal pattern also will be altered. What establishes the formal pattern will be three or more recurrences of a given arrangement of words, ordinarily in accord with a distinctive syntactic structure. Fewer than three such occurrences, e.g., of a given mode of formulating a thought, were not found by the framers to suffice to impart that patterned formulation that they proposed to use.

As I shall show here, very commonly in the Division of Purities the formulary or syntactic pattern will recur in groups of three or five, or multiples of three or five, examples. Obviously, the resort to highly formalized language-patterns facilitates memorization of materials. In so stating, I do not impose my own concerns of the framers or impute to them intentions I cannot demonstrate they held. We know, as a matter of fact, that the Mishnah was received and transmitted principally through the memories of professional tradition-memorizers, "people who repeat," or Tannas (the Aramaic word for repeat, TN', corresponding to the Hebrew, SNH). Accordingly, the patterns I shall here demonstrate to have characterized the formulation of the Mishnah assuredly served as mnemonics, though I should not wish to claim that that is the sole purpose behind the formal speech-patterns of the document. A routine glance at the other principal documents of the rabbinic canon will show that equivalent mnemonic considerations rarely characterize entire compositions, though patterned language will make an appearance in small units of completed discourse, e.g., occasional sayings or stories. The Tosefta, for its part, in no way follows the highly formalized and rigidly disciplined pattern of language characteristic of the Mishnah.

Since I claim that we recognize the subunits, or intermediate units of discourse, of tractates by reference to patterned language corresponding to and marking off consideration of distinctive topics, the focus of inquiry is clear. I have to take up those dimensions of linguistic patterning characteristic of already constituted units of discourse, I mean, the intermediate ones. I have also to deal with the smallest units of discourse and demonstrate that these too are patterned. Only by showing that both the intermediate and the smallest units of completed thought conform to syntactic or other linguistic rules shall I succeed in making my case. So in Chapter Two I show that intermediate units of discourse follow the rules I have outlined. That is, the authors so express ideas that a given principle or point is expressed in a repeated linguistic pattern, with the pattern changing when the topic shifts. In Chapters One and Three I show that the smallest whole units of thought, the building blocks of all else, conform to clearcut patterns.

When we come to the irreducible minima of discourse, those smallest possible units of discourse or cognitive units, that join words into intelligible sentences and sentences into intelligible propositions, we ordinarily deal with a brief paragraph made up of two parts, a protasis, which spells out a condition or a question, and an apodosis, which presents the rule governing the condition or the answer to the question. That is to say, the Mishnah is made up of many thousands of syllogisms, and sentences come together into meaningful propositions -- small paragraphs -- because they present in a systematic way logical propositions, ordinarily susceptible to reduction to a simple statement: If..., then..., or its equivalent. I deal with the mnemonic patterns of these cognitive units, as I said, in Chapters One and Three.

I first noticed the highly disciplined patterns dictating the way in which thoughts will come to expression as formal propositions (that is, as intelligible sentences) when I worked on the units of discourse in the Mishnah, and in other compositions of the rabbinic canon, in which names of authorities before 70 occur. These I called "the rabbinic traditions about the Pharisees." What I found was that, when I focused upon the smallest whole units of thought, sentences that comprised paragraphs (in simple language) or syllogisms that were whole and complete, a few rules governed. These rules, once memorized, made it exceedingly easy to reconstruct part of the whole units of thought, whatever their content. At that state in my work, I dealt only with the apodosis of the whole units of thought, that is, the "then..." of the "if..., then...,"-construction. What I found was the statement of a condition or a problem, in which, at that time, I discerned no pattern, followed by X says..., Y says.... The attributives, just now cited, would very regularly be followed by words that would recur many times over, always as matched opposites, e.g., "unclean/clean," "prohibited/permitted," and the like. Seeing the same pattern hundreds of times, I realized that I could construct in memory, simply knowing a handful of basic rules, pretty much any dispute in the corpus of materials attributed to the authorities before 70, and, without exception, any dispute assigned to the names of the Houses of Shammai and Hillel. Of course I was by no means the first to recognize the existence of such fixed patterns, since the framers of the Talmuds themselves noticed them and asked why the House of Shammai (nearly) always takes precedence, in reports of disputes, over the House of Hillel. But in a great many details, and in the grasp of the whole, I believe I was the person who first understood the working of the system.

It was one thing to perceive something so superficial as fixed patterns in apodoses, since these are few, brief, highly formal, and commonplace. So I saw little difficulty in focusing upon the apodosis as a focus of mnemonic patterning. I was puzzled by the much more difficult problem of the protasis of the syllogistic statements of the Mishnah. I simply did not grasp where and how the statement of the condition or problem to be disposed of exhibited a parallel set of mnemonic patterns. The reason, I now recognize, was that I was working, in connection with the Rabbinic Traditions about the Pharisees, and, for two years more, with Eliezer ben Hyrcanus (Lieden, 1973: E. J. Brill) I-II, only with bits and pieces of intermediate units of discourse ("chapters"). That is to say, because I followed the lines indicated by the occurrences of named authorities, I violated the lines of formal structure of the Mishnah as a whole. I neglected the formally definitive patterns of the intermediate units of discourse. I could never have recognized those patterns, at least, on the basis of systematic and detailed inquiry, by working as I did.

The recognition of intermediate units of discourse, how they found distinct definition in patterned language used in fixed and repetitious statements of a principle or rule in a single syntactic structure, came exactly where it should. When I turned from studies of individual names pursued across the boundaries of the components of the rabbinic canon, I took up studies of individual documents, following the boundaries of a single composition within the canon. Then, and only then, was I able to perceive the syntactic patterns as they repeated themselves, on the one side, and shifted with a change in the topical program, on the other. What I perceived was interplay of rhetorical and topical programs. How so? The logic of a syllogism reached the surface through its recurrent topical expression. The rhetoric utilized in that expression would, in context, prove distinctive to that distinct logical-topical construct. When I had penetrated into that deep structure of discourse in which logic generated topic and topic dictated rhetoric, I also had reached to the center of the mnemonic structure of the Mishnah's intermediate building blocks, that is, the components of the tractates that constitute the principal ones. That, in summary, is the proposition of this book.

The order of chapters is clear. I deal first with the simplest mnemonic patterns, those characteristic of the apodosis. In order to show the mnemonics of the protasis, I have to prove two facts, as I have indicated. The first is the interplay among rhetoric, logic and topic, dealt with in Chapter Two. Here I show how groups of topical examples of a single logical point resort to a single rhetorical or syntactic pattern. Fore and aft will be groups of examples of some other point. These will be characterized by a different rhetorical or syntactic pattern. Then in Chapter Three I move further into the rhetorical data, with special reference to the "simple declarative sentence" and its differentiation into rhetorical patterns. Finally, in Chapter Four, I state what I believe to be the facts of mnemonics presented in the first three chapters.

As I have said, I make constant reference, in Chapter One to the Rabbinic Traditions about the Pharisees, III, and in Chapters Two and Three, to A History of the Mishnaic Law of Purities, I-XX, that is, my original presentation of the texts and analysis of their formal and legal contents. Readers with the patience to follow up my references in Vols. I-XX will see the full basis for the statements of this book. Others will be able to follow the main lines of argument, secure in the notion that I have done the analytical work. I base all of my conclusions upon an acutely-detailed inquiry into the texts at hand. At every point readers are encouraged to spot-check my observations.

My hope is that by representing the main points in an accessible volume such as this, I may gain that hearing for those findings that the original, somewhat obscure and prolix presentation did not enjoy. So I hope to contribute to some facts to the on-going discussion of the oral character of the literature of Judaism, facts that, in my view, warrant some consideration.

CHAPTER ONE
THE APODOSIS
THE EVIDENCE OF THE RABBINIC TRADITIONS ABOUT THE PHARISEES

i. Introduction

The smallest whole unit of discourse is made up of fixed, recurrent formulas, clichés, patterns, or little phrases, out of which whole pericopae, or large elements in pericopae, e.g. complete sayings, are constructed. Small units of tradition, while constitutive of pericopae, do not generate new sayings or legal problems, as do apophthegmatic formulae. That is, MRBH -- MRBH -- produces numerous sayings; say unclean -- say clean -- does not; rather, it merely serves as apodosis for a random protasis.

An example of part of a pericope composed primarily of recurrent formulas is as follows:

A basket of fruit intended for the Sabbath
House of Shammai declare exempt
And the House of Hillel declare liable.

The italicized words are not fixed formulas. And is redactional; the formulation of the statement of the problem does not follow a pattern. The Houses-sentences, by contrast, are formed of fixed, recurrent phrases, which occur in numerous pericopae. Similarly:

House of Shammai say ... House of Hillel say ...

are fixed small units, whether or not the predicate matches; when it balances, we have a larger unit of tradition composed of two small units:

1.	House of Shammai say,	2.	BKY YTN
3.	House of Hillel say,	4.	Not BKY YTN.

In this pericope, only the statement of the problem or protasis, not given, would constitute other than a fixed unit; House of Shammai/Hillel + say are complete units, and the opinions in the apodosis are others -- thus, as I said, a pericope, the apodosis of which is composed entirely of fixed, small units of tradition.

By definition these small formulas cannot be random, or they would not constitute formulas. Such small units are whole words, not syntactical or grammatical particles. They also are not mere redactional devices used to join together discrete pericopae in the later processes of collection and organization, such as $ma^{c}aseh$, SN'MR, ^{c}LYK

HKTWB'WMR, and similar connecting-words, editorial conventions, formulaic introductions to Scriptures, and other redactional clichés.

The most important fixed formula is: X says. Now it may seem that so routine a phrase cannot be regarded as a formula. But its form, sense and function here are absent in all other Jewish literature. It obviously is not the only or best possible way of introducing a quotation of a named master. The use of the present tense participle with regard to a named master is anti-historical. We find X says, but not X does, X writes, X decrees, X rules.

Unlike the noun-epithet formula found by Milman Parry in the Iliad and the Odyssey ("Studies in the Epic Technique of Oral Verse-Making. I. Homer and Homeric Style," Harvard Studies in Classical Philology 41, 1930, pp. 73-148; and "II. The Homeric Language as the Language of an Oral Poetry," ibid., 43, 1932, pp. 1-50), the formulas before us seldom exhibit a meter, nor is any fixed metrical value often an obvious formal consideration (except in Houses-pericopae), because of the plain fact that at the time of the rabbis people no longer used metric speech for prosaic purposes. But the Houses' syzygy supplies for the apodosis or predicate of the Houses' pericopae the same sort of balanced, therefore easy to memorize, elements. Parry's description applies without qualification: "Unless the language itself stands in the way, the poet ... of the Homeric poems has ... a noun-epithet formula to meet every regularly recurring need. And what is equally striking, there is usually only one such formula." Likewise, the tradent of the Houses' pericopae has a standard syzygy available for the apodosis of every regularly recurring legal problem and sometimes even uses an available syzygy where it does not closely fit the facts of the case. Organization of materials for each memorization says nothing about what lies in the historical background of the materials, only about what was intended for the future: from redaction onward, it may well have been planned that they would be learned by heart, therefore to begin with should be constructed to facilitate easy memorization. The syzygous construction of the Houses' apodosis is a literary convention of written materials. It constitutes a 'fixed formula' in literature available to us only in written form. More than this cannot be granted as fact.

ii. Syntactic Patterns in the Apodosis of Houses' Disputes

The Houses of Shammai and Hillel, that is, disciples of those masters, generally assumed to have flourished in the first half of the first century, gain the credit for approximately half of all pericopae attributed to authorities before A.D. 70 in the rabbinic traditions of the Mishnah and later writings.

All Houses-pericopae manifest order and balance and follow redactional patterns, or, at the very least, formulas. I shall not catalogue the several types of small units of tradition and other mnemonic patterns and list the pericopae in which they occur.

1. Fixed Opposites

Strictly speaking, we find fixed formulas only in the syzygies of the Houses-disputes' apodosis. The choices normally are consistent within, and appropriate to, the tractates in which they occur, e.g., unclean in the cleanness-order. They are as follows:

a. Liable vs Free (HYB/PTWR, MHYYBYN/PWTRYN)

1. Thought of heart   (Mekh. deR. Ishmael XV 49-55)
   [Speculative]
2. She who aborts on eve of eighty-
   first day -- sacrifice   (M. Ker. 1:6)
3. Sweet oil   (M. Dem. 1:3 [Tos. Dem. 1:26-7])
4. Excess of 'omer etc.   (Tos. Dem. 1:28)
5. Hallah   (y. Dem. 5:1)
6. Basket of fruit for Sabbath   (M. Ma. 4:2)
7. Sift by hand   (Tos. Ma. 3:10)
8. Flour paste, dumplings   (M. Hal. 1:6)

Unlike the Qumranian laws, we do not find the explication of the referent of HYB; what
must be done is either implicit in context or ignored. Penalties are not specified.

b. Unclean/Clean (TM' vs. THR, MTM'YN vs. MTHRYN)

1. Articles made of common nails   (M. Kel. 11:3 [Tos. Kel. B.M. 1:2])
2. Bride's stool that lost seat-boards   (M. Kel. 22:4)
   (+ Shammai with 'P)
3. Scroll covers with figures   (M. Kel. 28:4)
   (Reconstruction)
4. Outer surfaces of alum-vessel   (Tos. Kel. B.Q. 2:1)
   (Reconstruction)
5. Peat in oven   (Tos. Kel. B.Q. 6:18)
6. Shovel lost blade   (Tos. Kel. B.M. 3:8)
7. Mustard-strainer with two holes   (Tos. Kel. B.M. 4:16)
8. Stool fixed inside baking trough, etc.   (Tos. Kel. B.B. 1:12)
9. Wrapper for garments   (Tos. Kel. B.B. 4:9)
10. Girdle from side of garment   (Tos. Kel. B.B. 5:7-8 [M. Kel. 28:7])
11. Bottle used as plug for grave   (Tos. Ah. 15:9)
12. Cover up olives in cleanness vs.
    in uncleanness   (M. Toh. 9:7)
13. He places from baskets with clean
    vs. unclean hands   (M. Toh. 10-4)
14. Leaving vessels in public   (Tos. Toh. 8:9B-10)
15. Types of liquid   (M. Nid. 2:6)
16. Blood of gentile woman   (M. Nid. 4:3A, Tos. Nid. 5:5)

17. If immersed self next day and had
    connection and suffered flux   (M. Nid. 10:8)
    (Theoretical reconstruction)

18-19-20. Man shook tree etc.   (M. Maksh. 1:2-4 [Tos.
    Subject to law of If water be put   Maksh. 1:1-4])
    vs. not = unclean, clean
    (Three examples)

21-22. Water leaked into trough   (M. Maksh. 4:5 [Tos. Maksh.
    Subject to If water vs. not   2:6])
    (Two examples)

23. Lyings and sittings   (Tos. Zab. 1:3)

24. Song of Songs   (M. Yad. 3:5 [M.^{C}Ed. 5:3])

25.-26. Olives and grapes that turned hard   (M. ^{C}Uqs. 3:6)
    (Two examples)

27. Blood of carcass   (b. Ker. 21a)

28. Sin-offering-water that has served
    its purpose   (M. ^{C}Ed. 5:3)

c. Prohibit/Permit ('WSRYN vs. MTYRYN)

1. Se'ah of unclean heave-offering in
    a hundred of clean   (M. Ter. 5:4, Tos. Ter. 6:4)
        Better apodosis:
            Eliezer: Take up and burned
            Sages: Lost through scantiness

2. Work on night of 13th of Nisan   (M. Pes. 4:5)

3. Bringing back ladder   (Tos. Y.T. 1:8)

4. Remove doors of cupboard   (Tos. Y.T. 1:10B)

5. Empty vessels not on account of need   (Tos. Y.T. 1:11A)

6. Gifts on festival   (Tos. Y.T. 1:12)
        (In M. Bes., all equivalents use
        negative + permit)

7. Substitutes for substitutes of vows   (Tos. Nez. 1:1)

8. Harlot makes wheat into flour for alter   (b. Tem. 30b)

9. Egg from bird's carcass   (y. Bes. 1:1)

d. Unfit/Fit (KSR vs. PSWL, MKSYRYN vs. PWSLYN)

1. Old Sukkah   (M. Suk. 1:1)

2. Man's head and greater part of body
    in Sukkah and table in house   (M. Suk. 2:7)
        (Should be: YS' +/- L')

3. Citron of demai   (M. Suk. 3:5)

4-5. If performed <u>halisah</u>   (M. Yev. 1:4)

    (Two examples)

6. Woman has intercourse with minor

    son, <u>re</u> priesthood   (Tos. Sot. 4:7)

7. Sprinkled and poured out blood once   (Tos. Zev. 4:9)

8. Slaughtered with reaping sickle

    KDRK HWLKTH   (M. Hul. 1:2)

9. One who forgets etc.   (M. Miq. 4:1)

    (Theoretical reconstruction)

To this list we may add YS' <u>vs</u>. L' YS', <u>he has, has not, fulfilled his obligation</u>:

1. Vowed without term and shaved on

    thirtieth   (Tos. Nez. 2:10)

2. See above, M. Suk. 2:7, no. 2.

We should have expected more extensive use of this syzygy.

e. <u>Midras/Teme-Met</u>

1. Trough for mixing mortar   (M. Kel. 20:2)

2. Leather bag or wrapper for purple wool (M. Kel. 26:6)

f. <u>Inside/Outside; Past/Future; Above/Below</u>

These are commonplace opposites of <u>meaning</u>. They occur as follows:

<u>Inside vs. Outside</u>:

1. Flesh of holy of holies burned --

    inside/outside   (Sifra Sav 8:6, M. Sheq. 8:6)

2. Produce not fully harvested passed

    through Jerusalem -- eaten inside/

    outside   (M. M.S. 3:6-7)

    (Theoretical reconstruction)

3. Olive presses whose doors open inward

    and contained space outward   (M. M.S. 3:6, 7, 3:12; Tos. M.S.

                                      2:12)

4. Second-tithe made unclean -- redeemed

    and eaten inside <u>vs</u>. outside   (M. M.S. 3:9; Tos. M.S. 2:16)

5. Measure chest   (M. Kel. 18:1)

<u>Past vs. coming year (LS^{C}BR vs. L^{C}TYD LB')</u>

1. Pod   (Tos. Shev. 2:6)

Above vs. below:

1. ^CEruv for cistern   (M. ^CEruv. 8:6)

2. Balance of Meter

In some pericopae, the Houses' lemmas are balanced not only in the number of syllables of the introductory clause: House X say, House Y say, -- 5 vs. 5 -- but also in the exact meter of the apodoses, whether or not the actual words correspond and contrast, as above. These are metrical syzygies, e.g. six syllables vs. six syllables. One may observe that TM'/THR, HYB/PTWR, and some other fixed opposites also are metrically balanced.

1. TRWMT ^CSMN BHM vs. 'YN TRWMTN TRWMH   (M. Ter. 1:4)
    6 vs. 6 (?)

2. See M. M.S. 3:6-7 part 3: BYRWSM vs BKL MQWM
    4 vs. 4

3. Who is a child?
    KL S'YNW YKWL LRKWB ^CL KTPYW SL'BYW
    vs. KL S'YNW YKWL L'HWZ BYDW SL'BYW

4-5-6. HLW vs. HZQ -- Yahaloqu vs. behezqatan   (M. Yev. 4:3, M. Ket. 8:6,
                                                     M. B.B. 9:8-9)
    4 vs. 4 (Four exempla) -- HLW vs. HZ' = L vs. Z

7. SLSYM vs. THYLH   (M. Naz. 3:6)
    3 vs. 3

8. (H)RSWT BYDW vs. ('YN) SWM^CYN LW   (Tos. Ket. 8:9)
    4(5) vs. 4(5)

9. YHB<u>L</u> vs. YHB<u>R</u>   (M. Kel. 14:2 [Tos. Kel. B.M.
                                                     4:5])

10. MSY<u>TB</u>R vs. MSY<u>QS</u>R   (M. Kel. 20:6)
    (^CAqiba: MSYQB)

11. ^CWMDT vs. SRWRH   (Tos. Kel. B.M. 11:3)
    3 vs. 3

12. KSYPTH vs. KSYTHYL   (M. Oh. 7:3)
    4 vs. 4
    (Note: Agreement uses both roots:
    PTH vs. THL = P vs. L)

13. 'RB^CH vs. KL SHW'   (M. Oh. 11:1)
    3 vs. 3

14. (MSYZY'W) Z^CZT HM^CTN vs. (MSYTHBRW)
    SLSH ZH LZH   (M. Toh. 9:1)
    6 vs. 6

15. TSMYS vs. LYLH   (M. Nid. 2:4)
    2 vs. 2

16. YSBR vs. Y^CRH   (M. Maksh. 4:4)

17. MSYSWDW vs. MSYMWTW   (M. ^CUqs. 3:8)
18. MSYHRHR vs. MSYRSQ   (M. ^CUqs. 3:11)
     5 vs. 5, in both nos. 17 and 18

Another very close balance of words is as follows:

19. House of Shammai say, One might [say]
     YHWG 'DM BYWM TWB
     TLMWD LWMR 'K
     BMW^CD 'TH HWGG W'YN 'TH HWGG BYWM TWB
     House of Hillel say, One might [say]
     YHWG 'DM BSBT
     TLMWD LWMR 'K
     BYWM TWB 'TH HWGG W'YN 'TH
     HWGG BSBT   (Sifra Emor 15:5)
          The difference is YWM TWB vs. MW^CD
          and SBT vs. YWM TWB -- 4 vs. 4, or,
          in effect, MW^CD vs. SBT, 2 vs. 2.

3. Balance of Meter and Change of Letter

In the following pericopae, we find metric syzygies of word order and a single change of a letter:

1. HZR MQWM BRK vs. BRK MQWM ZKR = 1,2,3
     vs. 3,2,1   (M. Ber. 8:7)
     H vs. Z.
2. HZR 'KL BYRWSLM vs. PDH 'KL BKL MQWM   (M. M.S. 3:6-7)

Thus: 1.   HZR vs. PDH
         2.   'KL = 'KL
         3.   4 metres vs. 4 metres

iii. Syntactical and Morphological Changes Equivalent in Function to Recurrent Formulas

Other mnemonic patterns, some of them very common, function like small units of tradition, in that they set up balanced opposites. But what is set in opposition is not the choice of words for the apodosis, as in ii 1. a-f, or balances of different words in identical meter, as in ii. 2,3. Rather, first, the arrangement of words will be changed in a single detail, so that one needs merely to remember which of two words comes first in the lemma of which House; or, second, the words will be identical, but the syntactical elements will change, e.g. and vs. or; or, third, the Houses' opinions will be identical, except that one will have a negative; or, fourth, one will make a negative statements and the other will permit. Fifth, while 'P is frequently a redactional device, sometimes it functions much like a mnemonic, such as permit; or like a change in order order; or like and vs. or.

1. Tense + Number

1. Did create light vs. does create lights   (M. Ber. 8:5)

2. Distinction vs. No. Distinction (And vs. Or)

The difference between the Houses will be represented either by and vs. or (= not vs. and), with all elements repeated in each lemma; or by the statement of a distinction in the first lemma, followed by this and this ... in the second; or one element will include only ... not, the other (both ... and).

1. Leaven/olive, bread/date vs. all (ZH WZH) etc.   (Sifre Deut. 131, M. Bes.
                                                         1:1, Tos. Y.T. 1:4)
2. Water plants until the New Year -- foliage
    and it drips on the root vs. both on foliage
    and on root   (Tos. Shev. 1:5)
3. All ten vs. ten/eleven   (M. M.S. 4:8)
4. Redeem with money vs. all same whether money
    or produce (BYN...BYN...)   (M. M.S. 5:7)
5. Redeem produce with coins in Jerusalem:
    This and this are Second Tithe vs. coins
    as they were and fruits as they were   (Tos. M.S. 3:14-15)
6. Grapes vs. wine, grapes and wine   (Tos. M.S. 5:17)
7. Hot water, not food vs. hot water and food   (M. Shab. 3:1)
8. Only in case of need vs. in case of need
    and not in case of need   (Tos. Shab. 14:1)
9. Side-post and/or cross-beam   (M. ^{C}Eruv. 1:2 [b. ^{C}Eruv. 6a,
                                                         y. ^{C}Eruv. 1:1])
10. Loosen and remove vs. loosen or remove   (M. Suk. 1:7)
11. Immerse all vs. vessels before, men on Sabbath   (M. Bes. 2:2)
12. Bring peace-offerings and not lay hands vs.
    bring and lay   (M. Bes. 2:3)
13. Only betrothed vs. betrothed and married
14. Husband, not YBM vs. husband and YBM
15. In presence vs. in presence and not in presence
16. Before court vs. before court and not before court (M. Yev. 13:1)
17. Adolescent and not child vs. both
18. Three times vs. even four/five   (M. Yev. 13:1)
        (Theoretical continuation)

19. Saw others eating figs: permitted <u>and</u>
    prohibited <u>vs.</u> <u>both</u> permitted   (M. Ned. 3:2)
20. Three betrothe: <u>two</u> witnesses <u>and one</u>
    agent <u>vs.</u> <u>all</u> three agents   (Tos. Qid. 4:1)
21. How long is novitiate of <u>haver</u>: Liquids,
    thirty days, garment, twelve months
    <u>vs.</u> <u>both</u> (ZH WZH) thirty days   (b. Bekh. 30b)
22. YHBL <u>and</u> YHBR <u>vs.</u> YHBL <u>or</u> YHBR   (Tos. Kel. B.M. 4:5, 11:7)
23-24-25. All become unclean <u>vs.</u> oven unclean
    <u>and</u> house clean   (M. Oh. 5:1-4)
        (Three examples)
26. Increase <u>and</u> overflow <u>vs.</u> increase <u>or</u> overflow   (M. Miq. 1:5 [Tos. Miq. 1:7,
                                                                         10])

27. Set or left in forgetfulness -- both invalid
    <u>vs.</u> <u>only set</u> invalid   (M. Miq. 4:1)

3. Reversal of Word-Order

Another common mnemonic pattern assigns all elements of the apodosis to both
Houses, but then reverses the order of the elements, as follows:

1. Houses: Heave-offering vetches -- soak, rub,
    give as food in cleanness   (M. M.S. 2:4 [Tos. M.S. 2:1])
        (Shammai and ^CAqiba out of balance)
2. Re'iyyah -- two silver, SMHH -- M^CH <u>vs.</u>
    Re'iyyah -- M^CH, SMHH -- two silver   (Sifre Deut. 143, M. Hag.
                                                                    1:2)
3. Day/wine <u>vs.</u> wine/day   (M. Ber. 8:1)
4. Wash/mix <u>vs.</u> mix/wash   (M. Ber. 8:2)
5. Clean/wash <u>vs.</u> wash/clean   (M. Ber. 8:4)
6. Wine/food <u>vs.</u> food/wine   (M. Ber. 8:8)
7. Sweet oil in right hand and wine in left
    hand <u>vs.</u> wine in right hand and sweet oil
    in left hand   (Tos. Ber. 5:27)
8. KL 'HD <u>vs.</u> 'HD [^CL]HKL
        (1, 2 <u>vs.</u> 2, 1)   (Tos. Ber. 5:30, b. Ber. 53a)
9. Oil/myrtle <u>vs.</u> myrtle/oil   (b. Ber. 34b)
10. KL 'HD <u>vs.</u> 'HD [^CL] HKL --plots sown with
    grain-Pe'ah   (M. Pe'ah 3:1)
        (1, 2 <u>vs.</u> 2, 1)
11. [^CEruv] LKL 'HD <u>vs.</u> 'HD [L]KL[M]   (M. ^CEruv. 6:6)
12. Day/wine <u>vs.</u> wine/day   (M. Pes. 10:2 [Tos. Pisha
                                                                    10:2-3])

13. Measure of re'iyyah greater than of hagigah
    vs. hagigah, than re'iyyah   (Tos. Hag. 1:4)
    (= No. 2 above)
14. Heaven/each vs. earth/heaven   (b. Hag. 12a)
    (Speculative)

4. Statements of Law +/- Negative

The single most common matched pattern assigns all elements of the apodosis to
both Houses and differentiates only by the inclusion of the negative -- 'YN or L' -- in one
House's lemma.

1. BWDQYN +/- 'YN   (Mekh. Pisha III 209-216)
    (Speculative)
2. Vintage for vat: HWKSR +/- 'YN   (b. Shab. 15a)
    [Should be: TM'/THR]
3. To lay (LSMK) +/- L'   (M. Hag. 2:2)
4. Baby born circumcized -- draw blood of
    covenant +/- 'YN   (Sifra Tazri^{c}a 1:5, Tos.
                                                  Shab. 3:18)
5. Field prepared -- eat fruit in Sabbatical
    year +/- 'YN   (Sifra Behar 1:5A, M. Shev.
                                                  4:2)
6. Eat produce by favor +/- not by favor   (Sifra Behar 1:5B)
7. Exempted what was cooked in pot +/- L'   (y. Ber. 6:5)
8. Forgotten sheaf +/- 'YN (twice)   (M. Pe'ah 6:2-3)
9. Ownerless vs. not ownerless unless also to
    rich = HBQR +/- 'YN   (M. Pe'ah 6:1)
10. Grapes of fourth-year vineyard -- 'YN Fifth +
    removal vs. YS; YS gleanings + cluster vs.
    KLW LGT   (M. Pe'ah 7:6, Tos. M.S.
                                                  5:17)

    (Not exact.)
11. He who plants row of five vines -- vineyard
    +/- 'YN   (M. Kil. 4:5)
12. Caperbush in vineyard -- Mixed seeds +/- 'YN   (Tos. Kil. 3:17)
13. Give heave-offering +/- 'YN   (Tos. Ter. 2:5)
14. Give heave-offering +/- 'YN   (Tos. Ter. 3:14)
15. Give heave-offering +/- 'YN   (Tos. Ter. 3:16)
    (And Scriptural arguments, Num. 18:27 vs.
    Lev. 27:30)
16. Doubtful heave-offering + burn +/- 'YN   (y. Pes. 3:6)

17. Heave-offering from several jars, open and
    empty +/- 'YN [= empty only]   (M. M.S. 3:13, Tos. M.S.
                                                   2:18)

18. Cooked food: remove vs. it is as if already
    removed (Conjectural: development of
    do not remove)   (M. M.S. 5:6)

19. Less than egg's bulk renders unclean +/- not   (M. ^COrl. 2:4-5)

20. That ^Ceruv is an ^Ceruv +/- 'YN   (b. ^CEruv. 48b)

21. Prepare ^Ceruv with wine for Nazirite
    etc. +/- 'YN   (b. ^CEruv. 30a)

22. Convert on day before Passover: Not require
    sprinkling vs. requires   (M. Pes. 8:8)
        (Theoretical formulation. Actual: immerses
        and eats vs. he that separates)

23. Burn piggul, notar, and unclean meat
    together +/- 'YN   (b. Pes. 15b)

24. Return limbs +/- 'YN   (Tos. Pisha 7:2)

25. Egg laid on festival day -- eaten +/- 'YN   (M. Bes. 1:1)

26. Bring burned-offering for festival +/- 'YN   (b. Bes. 19a [vs. M. Bes. 2:3])

27. Scattered in enclosure, gathered in field --
    bring +/- 'YN   (Tos. Y.T. 3:10 [M. Bes. 4:2])

28. Day for slaughtering is after Sabbath +/- 'YN (M. Hag. 2:4)

29. Laying on of hands not in ordinary manner has
    been permitted +/- L'   (y. Hag. 2:3)

30. Marries and +/- 'YN takes Ketuvah   (M. Yev. 15:3)

31. Co-wives went and married -- are fit +
    progeny are fit +/- 'YN   (Tos. Yev. 1:7)

32. Woman inherits goods before betrothal --
    sell, give away, etc. +/- 'YN   (M. Ket. 8:1)

33. Absolution for oath +/- 'YN   (b. Ned. 28a)

34. Nazir +/- 'YN   M. Naz. 1:2)

35. HQDS +/- 'YN   M. Naz. 5:1-2)

36. Nazir +/- 'YN   (M. Naz. 5:5)
        (Slight variations)

37. Testify by echo +/- 'YN   (Tos. Nez. 1:1)

38. Bald Nazirite passes razor over head +/- 'YN   (b. Naz. 46b)

39. Man imposes vow on son +/- 'YN   (Tos. Nez. 3:17)

40. All Nazirites vs. only Nazir who   (Tos. Nez. 3:19)
        (Variation: 'YN...'L'...)

41. Takes Ketuvah and drinks +/- 'YN   (M. Sot. 4:2)
        (Compare no. 30.)

42. Divorce and changed mind -- rendered wife
    ineligible to priest +/- L'

43. Divorce and spent night -- need second
     Get +/- 'YN   (M. Git. 8:8-9)
44. Middle group goes down +/- 'YN   ((Tos. Sanh. 13:3)
     (Theoretical reconstruction)
45. Piggul and Karet, piggul not Karet   (Tos. Zev. 4:9)
     (Close to and/or)
46. Fowl comes up with cheese +/- L'   (M. Hul. 8:1, Tos. Hul. 8:2-3)
47. Sanctifies property and intends to divorce
     wife -- may bring her back +/- 'YN   (Tos. ^CArakh. 4:5)
48. Consecration in error is consecration +/- 'YN   (b. ^CArakh. 23a)
49. Added Fifth to additional payment +/- 'YN   (Tos. ^CArakh. 4:22)
50. Measure empty-space +/- 'YN   (Tos. Kel. B.M. 8:1)
51-52-53. If man over split, does he bring in
     uncleanness +/- 'YN   (M. Oh. 11:3, 4, 5)
     (Three examples)
54. Search for Nazirite +/- 'YN   (M. Oh. 18:4)
55. Olives left to grow soft -- MWKSRYN +/- 'YN   (M. Toh. 9:5)
56. Immerse vessels in rain-steam vs. 'YN   (M. Miq. 5:6b)
57. Immerse hot water in cold +/- 'YN   (M. Miq. 10:6)
58. Needs immersion at end of purifying +/- 'YN   (M. Nid. 10:3)
59. Liable to offering +/- 'YN   (M. Nid. 10:7)
60-61. Serve as connector +/- 'YN   (M. T.Y. 1:1)
     (Two examples)
62. Layer of jelly -- connector +/- 'YN   (Tos. T.Y. 2:3)
63. Needs to broach +/- 'YN   (M. Maksh. 1:1)

5. Negative Statement + Permit

A pattern closely related to the foregoing supplies a full, negative statement to one side, then has the other side permit, or vice versa:

1.   Not sell ploughing heifer vs. permit   (M. Shev. 5:8)
2.   Not sell field vs. permit   (Tos. Shev. 4:5B)
3.   Not sell Seventh Year produce for coins vs. permit   (Tos. Shev. 6:19)
4.   Not change selas vs. permit   (M. M.S. 2:7)
5.   Do not plant vs. permit   (Tos. M.S. 5:20)
6.   Not soak ink etc. unless time to be wholly
     soaked while still day vs. permit
7.   Not put bundles of flax in over etc. vs. permit
8.   Not spread nets vs. permit
9.   Not sell to gentile vs. permit
10. Not give hides to tanner vs. permit   (M. Shab. 1:4-8)
11. Pharisee-Zab not eat with outsider vs. permit   (Tos. Shab. 1:14)
12. Not kill louse vs. permit   (Tos. Shab. 16:21)

13.	Send letter on Wednesday vs. permit	(y. Shab. 1:9)
14.	Not burn clean meat with unclean vs. permit	(Tos. Pisha 1:6)
15.	Do not remove ladder vs. permit	(M. Bes. 1:2)
16.	Not take off cupboard doors vs. permit	
17.	Not lift up pestle vs. permit	
18.	Not put hide before treading-place vs. permit	
19.	Not carry out child vs. permit	
20.	Not take dough-offering vs. permit	(M. Bes. 1:3-6)
21.	Not heat water vs. permit	(M. Bes. 2:4)
22.	Not bake thick bread on Passover vs. permit	(b. Bes. 22b)
23.	Permit co-wives to brothers vs. prohibit	(M. Yev. 1:4)
24.	Man divorces with old bill of divorce vs. prohibit	(M. Git. 8:4)
25.	Israelite not numbered with priest for firstling vs. permit	(M. Bekh. 5:2, Tos. Bekh. 3:15-16)

6. 'P in Second Lemma

'P normally serves redactional, not substantive purposes. Sometimes, however, it introduces an actual opinion, thus adding an item to a list, indicating a contrary opinion (= permit) and the like.

1.	'P adds the Shammaite opinion, with the Hillelite lemma out of balance	(M. ^{c}Orl. 2:4-5)
2.	Also like water of fenugreek etc.	(Sifra Tazri^{c}a 3:6 [compare M. Nid. 2:6])
3.	Also what was cooked in pot	(M. Ber. 6:5)
4.	(Not ownerless unless) also to rich	(M. Pe'ah 6:1)
5.	Sell olives on to haver vs. also to one who pays tithes	(M. Dem. 6:6)
6.	Hullin vs. 'P M^{c}SR	(M. Hag. 1:3 [Tos. Hag. 1:4])
7.	Vow in all except oath vs. even oath	
8.	Not be first vs. even first	
9.	Only matter vs. even not	(M. Ned. 3:4)
10.	Also siphon is clean	(M. Kel. 9:2)
11.	Intention before vs. even after	(M. Oh. 7:3)
12.	Cover up in cleanness vs. 'P in uncleanness	(M. Toh. 9:7)
13.	KMG^{c} TM' MT vs. 'P KTM'MT	(M. Nid. 10:6)
14.	'P porridge etc. ('P here is connector)	(M. Maksh. 5:9)

iv. Differences in Word-Choice

In a few instances, no real dispute seems to have separated the Houses. Juxtaposing their opinions, which use different words for pretty much the same thing, seems to suggest the presence of a difference where there is only a distinction in word choice, as in nos. 1, 2, 4, 6, 12(?), and 24. In other instances, the differences in word-choice evidently are significant and indicate a substantive dispute, as in nos. 3, 5, 7, 8, 9, 10, 11, 13, 14, 15, 16, 17, 18, 19, 20, 21, 22, and 23. In none of these does a metrical balance appear to have been a consideration in the formulation of a dispute.

1. Hin vs. qab -- Hillel/Shammai   (M. ^{C}Ed. 1:3A)
2. ^{C}T vs. PQYDH -- Shammai/Hillel   (M. ^{C}Ed. 1:1)
3. Table vs. cushion   ((M. Ber. 8:3)
4. Three furrows of ploughed land vs. width of
   Sharon yoke   (M. Kil. 2:6)
5. Measure from root vs. from wall   ((M. Kil. 6:1)
6. Sow tree-planted field until: so long as
   benefits produce vs. Pentecost   (M. Shev. 1:1)
7. Thin out olive trees in seventh year --
   Raze vs. uproot   (M. Shev. 4:4)
8. Dig up arum with wooden rakes vs. metal spades   (M. Shev. 5:4)
9. Unclean cask of heave-offering -- pour out
   vs. sprinkle   (b. Pes. 20b)
10. All the sela coins vs. sheqel, silver, sheqel, copper   (M. M.S. 2:8,9)
11. Raise up bones etc. from table vs. take entire
    table   (M. Shab. 21:3)
         (Also: singular vs. plural)
12. Reach home vs. reach house nearest wall   (b. Shab. 19a)
13. Search two rows: outermost vs. on the whole
    surface   (M. Pes. 1:1)
14. NDBH vs. HLYN   (M. Sheq. 2:3)
15. Fourth vs. mouthful   (b. Yoma 80a)
16. Continue (QYM) vs. put away (YS')   (M. Yev. 3:1, Tos. Yev. 5:1)
         (Theoretical form: M'MR + QDS +/- 'YN)
17. Two males vs. male and female   (M. Yev. 6:6 [Tos. Yev. 8:4])
         (Similar to distinction vs. no distinction)
18. When does husband inherit: womanhood
    vs. huppah   (b. Yev. 89b)
19. Bride as she is vs. lovely etc.   (b. Ket. 17a)
20. Inquired vs. vowed   (Tos. Nez. 3:19)
21. DBR vs. ^{C}RWH -- grounds for divorce
    (based on Deut. 24:1)   (M. Git. 9:10)
         (Two vs. two)
22. Denar vs. perutah   (M. Qid. 1:1)
23. MQNH vs. MDYH   (b. Hul. 104b)
24. ^{C}SMYM vs. GWYH   (M. ^{C}Ed. 1:7)
         (+ Shammai)
         (Perhaps: 3 vs. 3)

v. Number-Sequences

While number-sequences prove to be common, only 2 <u>vs.</u> 1 or <u>vice versa</u> tends to recur in a significant number of pericopae. Also a descending scale, e.g. 10, 9, 8, 7, or an ascending one, e.g., 2, 3, 4, appears more than episodically. The other sequences seem to come at random and to depend upon the substance of the laws under discussion, e.g., nos. 8 (derived from exegesis), 15, 16, 18, 33. Occasionally, we see opposed units of measurement, with the same number, e.g., no. 28.

1. 3 <u>vs.</u> 9 -- Hillel, Shammai   (M. ^CEd. 1:3A)

2. 12 <u>vs.</u> 36 -- Hillel, Shammai   (Tos. ^CEd. 1:3)

3. 1 <u>vs.</u> 2 -- Shammai, Hillel: <u>qab</u> for Hallah
    <u>vs.</u> two <u>qabs</u>   (M. ^CEd. 1:3)

4. 3/3/3 <u>vs.</u> 3/3/3 + 1/1/1 -- Hananiah Prefect
    of the Priests, Ishmael, and sages   (M. Men. 10:1)

5. 16/36/72 -- colors of leprosy-signs -- Hananiah
    Prefect of Priests, Dosa, ^CAqavya   (M. Neg. 1:4)

6. 3 <u>vs.</u> 4 -- how many tassels in <u>sisit</u> -- House
    of Hillel, then House of Shammai   (Sifre Num. 115, Deut. 234)

7. 4 <u>vs.</u> 3 -- how many tassels House of Shammai
    <u>vs.</u> House of Hillel   (b. Bekh. 39b-41a, b. Men.
                                                              41b)

8. 2 <u>vs.</u> 5 -- sheep liable to fleece   (M. Hul. 11:2, Sifre Deut.
                                                              166)

9. 10 <u>vs.</u> 9, 8 <u>vs.</u> 7 -- benedictions for New Year
    on Sabbath   (Tos. R. H. 2:17, Tos. Ber.
                                                              3:13)

10. 2, 3 <u>vs.</u> 3, 4   (M. Pe'ah 1:5)

11. Vineyard patch -- 24 <u>vs.</u> 16; outer space of
    vineyard -- 16 <u>vs.</u> 12   (M. Kil. 4:1)

12. Sows within four cubits of vineyard
    forfeits -- 1 <u>vs.</u> 2   (M. Kil. 4:5)

13. Measurement of dirt -- 10 <u>vs.</u> 6   (Tos. Kil. 4:11B)

14. Measure of heave-offering -- 20/40/50
    <u>vs.</u> 40/50/60   (M. Ter. 4:3)

15. When make vat unclean -- after <u>first vs.</u>
    <u>second</u> [tithe is taken]   (Tos. Ter. 3:12)
        (Not comparable to the others.)

16. Hanukkah -- start with 8 <u>vs.</u> 1   (b. Shab. 21b)

17. ^C<u>Eruv-tavshilin</u> -- 2 <u>vs.</u> 1   (M. Bes. 2:1, Tos. Y.T. 2:4)

18. First <u>vs.</u> fifteenth of Shevat   (M. R.H. 1:1)
        (Not comparable to the others.)

19. Overturn couch -- 3 <u>vs.</u> 1   (Tos. M.Q. 2:9)

20. Vow no intercourse -- 2 <u>vs.</u> 1   (M. Ket. 5:6)

21. Nursing mother remarry -- 24 <u>vs.</u> 98   (b. Ket. 60a-b)

22. How much blotted out -- 1 <u>vs.</u> 2   (y. Sot. 3:3)

23. Placings in sin-offering: 2 <u>vs.</u> 1   (M. Zev. 4:1)

24. Length of shafts -- 7 <u>vs.</u> 8, 9 <u>vs.</u> 10   (M. Kel. 29:8 [Tos. Kel. B.B.
7:4])

25. How much lacking in backbone -- 2 <u>vs.</u> 1   (M. Oh. 2:3)

26. Uncleanness inside -- vessels outside -- how

     bit split -- 4 <u>vs.</u> <u>any amount</u>   (M. Oh. 11:1)

27. Place for rod -- <u>any amount</u> <u>vs.</u> one   (M. Oh. 13.4)

28. Fore-court of tomb -- 4 <u>amot</u> <u>vs.</u> 4 <u>tefahim</u>   (M. Oh. 15:8)

29. Its thickness <u>vs.</u> one <u>tefah</u>   (Tos. Ah. 14:4)

30. 2 + 1 <u>vs.</u> 1 + 1   (Tos. Ah. 16:6)

31. From <u>third</u> row <u>vs.</u> from <u>second</u> row   ((Tos. Par. 5:1)

32. Come of age: 20 <u>vs.</u> 18   (M. Nid. 5:9)

33. Minor married --

     a) 4 nights <u>vs.</u> <u>wound heals</u>

     b) 1 <u>vs.</u> 4   (M. Nid. 10:1 [Tos. Nid.
9:7:9])

34. Makes void -- 2 <u>vs.</u> 1   (M. Zab. 1:2)

vi. <u>Houses-Disputes Not in Precise Balance</u>

In the following pericopae, we discern no balance in the formulations of the Houses-opinions. The lack of contrasting meter or syzygous word-choice in some instances is readily explained, however, for the subject-matter of the legal disputes or the substance of the opinions generally excludes the possibility of choosing words other than those before us, e.g., nos. 2, 4, 5, 13, 14, 16, 17, 25, 26. Even here, however, we find fixed lemmas, e.g. <u>after usual fashion</u> does not contrast with <u>pounded with pestle</u> or <u>pick pulse</u> (nos. 6, 7), but it does constitute a cliché. Likewise, no. 1 depends upon a cliché for the Shammaite opinion; the rest of the opinions balance with one another. As we observed, one could not have phrased the Shammaite opinion in the fixed terms of the Hillelites or ^CAqiba's, because, to begin with, it is variable. Nos. 2 and 4 rely on Scriptures. Nos. 3, 13, 22, and 24 are examples of unbalanced disputes which might have been formulated in the more conventional way. Some of the Houses' lemmas are scarcely related to one another, though they address themselves to the same legal problem, e.g., nos. 15, 19, 21. No. 2 is anomalous. All pericopae, however, do exhibit the standard structural balance, <u>House X say vs. House Y say.</u>

1. YLQH BHSR WYTR <u>vs.</u> KS^CT HWS'H + ^CAqiba:
     KS^CT TBY^CH   (Sifra Vayiqra 13:13,
M. B.M. 3:12)

2. How far recite Hallel + Ps. 114:8   (M. Pes. 10:8 [b. Pes. 117a =
Ps. 114:1 vs. Ps. 115:1])

3. Not sell leaven to gentile unless consumed
     before Passover <u>vs.</u> As long as Jew may eat,

he may sell it.   (b. Shab. 18b)

    (Better: +/- not.)

4. Where shake lulav + Ps. 118:1, 25A, 25B   (M. Suk. 3:9)

5. Not take pigeons vs. stands and says   (M. Bes. 1:3, Tos. Y.T. 1:8)

6. Spices pounded with pestle etc.
    vs. after usual fashion   (M. Bes. 1:7, Tos. Y.T. 1:15-17)

7. Pick pulse and eat edible parts
    vs. after usual fashion   (M. Bes. 1:8, Tos. Y.T. 1:21)

8. Send MNWT vs. send cattle etc.   (M. Bes. 1:9)

9. Cover up blood with dust vs. ashes are dust   (b. Hul. 88b)

10. Pishon the camel-driver   (b. Yev. 107b)
    (Debate on precedent)

11. We have heard no tradition vs. it is all one   (M. Yev. 15:2)

12. Co-wives free from marriage and betrothal etc. (Tos. Yev. 1:7)

13. Vow not to suckle -- pull breast vs. compel suckle   (b. Ket. 59b)

14. Testimony at variance vs. two included in five (M. Naz. 3:7 [Tos. Mez. 3:1])

15. Half-slave, half-free -- how arrange work etc. (M. Git. 4:5)

16. Steal beam -- take down vs. estimate value   (Tos. B.Q. 9:5)

17. KML' MQDH vs. KDY SYNTL MN HHY WYMWT   (M. Oh. 2:3)

18. KML' MQDH vs. ^CD SYH' BMQWM 'HD ML'
    MQDH   (M. Oh. 13:1)

19. How gather grapes in grave-area   (M. Oh. 18:1)

20. What do they examine   (M. Oh. 18:8)

21. Connective for uncleanness but not for sprinkling
    vs. if sprinkled on kettle, sprinkled on lid, not
    vice versa   (M. Par. 12:10
                                [Tos. Par. 12:18])

22. Blood of woman after childbirth -- like spittle
    vs. conveys uncleanness wet or dry   (M. Nid. 4:3B)

23. NSYM MTWT NDWT vs. NDH MTH NDH   (M. Nid. 10:4)
    (See II, p. 302-307; six vs. six.)

24. Convey uncleanness vs. such a one is gluttonous (M. Nid. 10:8)

25. Like one that waits day vs. like one that has
    suffered pollution

26. Wholly Zab vs. conveys uncleanness to what he
    sits on etc.   (M. Zab. 1:1)

27. He who anoints pure oil etc.   (y. Ber. 8:3)

28. Tefillin in privy   (b. Ber. 23a)
    The Houses are not in balance, but the Hillelites
    and ^CAqiba do match: hand vs. garment.

vii. Summary of Mnemonic Patterns

We have isolated and characterized the following mnemonic phenomena:

Pericopae containing small units of tradition or following other disciplined
mnemonic forms   314

a) Fixed formulas   86

    1. Fixed opposites   66

        Liable vs. free   8

        Unclean vs. clean   28

        Prohibit vs. permit   9

        Unfit vs. fit   10

        Midras vs. Teme-Met   2

        Inside vs. outside (etc.)   7

    2. Balance of meter   18

    3. Balance of meter and change of   2
        single letter

b) Syntactical and morphological changes   152
    functionally equivalent to fixed formulas

    1. Tenses and numbers   1

    2. Distinction vs. no distinction   27
        (and vs. or)

    3. Reversal of word-order   14

    4. Statements of law +/- negative   61

    5. Negative statement + permit   25

    6. 'P in second lemma   14

c) Differences in word choice   24

d) Number-sequences   34

e) Houses-disputes not closely balanced   28
    (Structural balance only: X say vs. Y say)

Pericopae exhibiting no clear mnemonic pattern pertain primarily to named
masters other than Hillel, Shammai, and the Houses. Pericopae containing small
units of tradition or following other mnemonic forms concern the Houses alone.
Among the pericopae exhibiting mnemonic patterns of some sort, we find the
following distribution:

    Houses: 31 + 314 = 345

    Hillel + Shammai: 19

    Gamaliel + Simeon b. Gamaliel: 9

    Chains ending with Shammai-Hillel: 2

    Baba b. Buta: 1

    Joshua b. Gamala: 2

    Abba Joseph: 1

    Hananiah Prefect of the Priests: 3

    Simeon the Just: 2

Yose's: 4

Yohanan, High Priest: 1

Hanina b. Dosa: 1

Simeon b. Shetah: 2

Shema^ciah and Abtalion: 1

In addition, the sayings in Avot follow a redactional pattern. As to the pericopae without mnemonic patterns, we find the following distribution:

Simeon the Just: 4

Yose's: 2

Joshua b. Perahiah: 3

Judah b. Tabbai and Simeon b. Shetah: 9

Shema^ciah and Abtalion: 5

Shammai: 6

Hillel: 17

(Houses: 8 [All in structural balance, as noted])

Hillel and Shammai: 3

Gamaliel: 14

Simeon b. Gamaliel: 4

Baba b. Buta: 2

Hananiah Prefect of the Priests: 9

Rest scattered.

The Houses' and Hillel-and-Shammai-pericopae normally exhibit mnemonic patterns or are balanced in some way or another, and the pericopae of other names masters are apt not to be balanced or to exhibit mnemonic patterns. Since in the list of mnemonic pericopae are pericopae whose mnemonic pattern derives from redactional, and not substantive, considerations, the imbalance is more considerable than these figures suggest.

viii. Conclusion

The majority of pericopae in the rabbinic traditions about the Pharisees before 70, and nearly all of the corpus of Houses-materials within those traditions, exhibit mnemonic patterns, some formal, some of them substantive, precise, and striking. What inferences are to be drawn from the fact? Shall we conclude that the traditions were based upon orally formulated and transmitted materials?

On the face of it, that conclusion is unwarranted. Clearly many traditions before us were formulated so as to facilitate their memorization. But whether or not the redacted pericopae derive from originally oral materials is a question that obviously cannot be settled, one way or the other, by the character of materials which we have only in written form. The later theory of a dual Torah by itself is not pertinent. Qumranians, for one, had such a corpus of revealed materials external to

Scriptures, and they wrote down at least part of those materials. But even if various sects had traditions, and if those traditions were oral, it would not solve the problem, unless it can be shown that in behalf of such traditions was claimed not merely essential accuracy but exact verbal correspondence with what was originally stated by the authority standing behind them.

Such a claim to exact verbal correspondence is laid down in behalf of the Mishnah. The data we have examined, as well as those to come, show us the basis for the claim. That is, the text is so formulated as to be relatively easy to memorize.

Saul Lieberman describes the process of formulating and transmitting the Mishnah in "The Publication of the Mishnah" (Hellenism in Jewish Palestine. Studies in the Literary Transmission, Beliefs, and Manners of Palestine in the I Century B.C.E. -- IV Century C.E. [N.Y., 1950], pp. 83-99). He asks, Was the Mishnah published? That is, either did professional copyists hear it dictated and write it down? Or did an authentic original take written form, and was it then deposited in an archive? Some Jewish books were published in the second way, that is, they were written and deposited. However, Lieberman notes, "Since in the entire Talmudic literature we do not find that a book of the Mishnah was ever consulted in case of controversies or doubt concerning a particular reading, we may safely conclude that the compilation was not published in writing." Rabbis did possess written halakhot and comments, but they were private notes without legal authority, with no more authority than an oral assertion (p. 87).

The Mishnah was published in a different way: "A regular oral ... edition of the Mishnah was in existence, a fixed text recited by the Tannaim of the college. The Tanna (repeater, reciter) committed to memory the text of certain portions of the Mishnah, which he subsequently recited in the college in the presence of the great masters of the Law ... When the Mishnah was committed to memory and the Tannaim recited it in the college it was thereby published ..." The authority of the college-Tanna ("a word apparently first used for college-reciter in the time of ^{C}Aqiba," Lieberman, p. 88, n. 39) was that of a "published book" (p. 89).

What was the nature of that living book? "How was the mass of diverse material arranged and systematized before it was delivered to the Tanna, before he memorized it?" (p. 90) At the time of ^{C}Aqiba, the body of the Mishnah comprised only the opinions of the representatives of the Houses of Shammai and Hillel and their predecessors (p. 93). ^{C}Aqiba organized matters, sifting through the whole and crystalizing it in an exact and definite shape. His work resulted in the compilation of a new Mishnah (p. 93). Then the procedure was as follows: "The Master taught the new Mishnah to the first Tanna; afterwards he taught it to the second Tanna" and so on. After the Mishnah was systematized and the Tannaim knew it thoroughly be heart, they repeated it in the college in the presence of the master, who supervised the recitation and corrected it and gave it its final form (p. 93). The materials we have catalogued provide evidence in favor of the theory of the publication of the Mishnah advanced by Lieberman.

CHAPTER TWO

THE PROTASIS

1. THE INTERMEDIATE DIVISIONS OF THE MISHNAH "CHAPTERS" AND

THEIR DEMARCATION

i. Introduction

The entire discussion that follows in Chapters Two and Three is based upon my analysis of the Mishnah's Division of Purities (History of the Mishnaic Law of Purities [Leiden, 1974-1977] I-XX). Reference is made to comments on individual pericopes in those twenty volumes of translation and analysis.

Internal evidence proves that the arrangement of the Order of Purities into twelve principal divisions is fundamental to the redaction of the Mishnah. Once a primary theme shifts, we know that the redactors have completed their treatment of one subject and commenced that of another. We shall now ask whether the dissection, into intermediate divisions, of these same principal divisions is shown by internal evidence to be equivalently fundamental to the redaction of the document.

The delineation of these subdivisions -- "chapters" -- is not to be confused with the present boundaries of chapters in the manuscripts, because the latter cannot be shown on the basis of manuscript-evidence to be present at, and even prior to, the very point at which the Mishnah reaches ultimate redaction. The earliest manuscript-evidence derives from a much later period than the redaction of the Mishnah itself. Evidence in the Gemarot for the same reason cannot be asked to tell us about the educational program of the people who stand behind the Mishnah. Only internal literary and ideational traits of the document provide acceptable evidence on the Mishnah's redactional history. That is why we cannot confuse intermediate divisions within the chapters into which the Mishnah is presently divided. I therefore place quotation marks around "chapters" to distinguish intermediate divisions to be demarcated upon the basis of internal evidence from chapter-lines laid down in later manuscript-evidence. This latter evidence constitutes a post-facto commentary, imposed after the document had come into being.

Since we seek to discern the boundary-lines within the principal divisions of the Mishnah for which the redactors of the Mishnah bear responsibility, we ask for internal evidence about the aggregation of materials into intermediate divisions. We now know that if our Order were before us in undifferentiated columns of words, or were written in a single immense scroll, without any sort of divisions and subdivisions, we should readily discern twelve principal divisions simply by observing the shift from one primary theme or subject to another. Within the twelve divisions, what internal evidence permits us to differentiate the intermediate divisions, or sizable aggregations of completed cognitive units? What criteria, specifically, will emerge out of the fundamental character itself?

The first of two criteria derives from the nature of the principal divisions themselves: theme. That is, it is along thematic lines that the redactors organized vast corpora of materials into principal divisions, tractates. These fundamental themes themselves were subdivided into smaller conceptual units. The principal divisions, I have shown at great length, treat their themes in units indicated by the sequential unfolding of their inner logical structure. Accordingly, one established criterion for the deliberation of an aggregate of materials from some other, fore or aft, will be a shift in the theme, or predominant and characteristic concern, of a sequence of materials.

The second fundamental criterion is the literary character, syntactical and grammatical pattern, which differentiates and characterizes a sequence of primitive units of thought. Normally, when the subject changes, the mode of expression -- the formal or formulary character, the patterning of language -- will change as well. These two matters, theme and form, therefore must be asked to delineate for us the main lines of the intermediate or subdivisions of the Mishnah's principal divisions, the "chapters."

There are therefore four logical possibilities for the application of the two stated criteria, +A, +B, +A-B, -A+B, -A-B:

1. coherent themes expressed through coherent formulary patterns;
2. coherent themes lacking coherent formulary patterns;
3. coherent formulary patterns lacking coherent themes;
4. incoherent themes and incoherent formulary patterns.

In this case the only reason to imagine that we deal with a subdivision is that before and after said set of materials, which lacks coherence of theme and form, are sets which do exhibit traits of coherent theme and/or form, that is, subdivisions demarcated by one of the first possible combinations.

These logical possibilities generated by the two criteria in fact are to be refined against the character of the evidence itself.

We distinguish to begin with between two kinds of formulary patterns.

First is the pattern which is internal to the idea which is expressed and which predominates in the formulation of that idea, its linguistic formalization. If this pattern recurs for two or more cognitive units, then we have a formulary trait internal to the pattern of language of each element in a subdivision. Each and every cognitive unit within said subdivision will express its particular concept or thought in conformity with this common pattern, which therefore is to be designated as _internal_ to the whole. The recurrent pattern of syntax or language is both tradental and redactional, in that what is to be expressed is the work of those responsible for both the formulary and formalized character and the cognitive substance of the subdivision in all of its parts and as a whole.

Second is the pattern which is external to the idea which is expressed and superficial, and which occurs chiefly at the outset of a cognitive unit. The arrangement of words of said unit will ignore this external formulary trait. What is to be said can be, and is, stated without regard to the superficial trait shared among several cognitive units. Indeed, we may readily discern that the formulary trait of a series of cognitive units is external to the formulation of all of them, simply because each cognitive unit goes its own way, stating its ideas in its own form or formulary pattern, without any regard whatsoever for the formal traits of other units to which it is joined. The joining --

the shared language or formulary or formal pattern -- is therefore external to the several units. The present distinction, between internally-unitary formulary traits characteristic of a sequence of cognitive units, and externally-unitary formulary traits shared by a sequence of cognitive units, explains why the first of our four logical possibilities, +A +B (coherent themes, coherent forms), yields two analytical categories, sections ii and iii of the present chapter.

The second logical possibility, +A-B, requires no refinement. We observe that some clearcut sequences of cognitive units talk about the same distinctive subject, but make no effort to conform to a discernible pattern of language. Section iv catalogues those subdivisions.

Occasionally we discern subdivisions which are differentiated by formulary patterns but which go over many legal themes, that is, -A+B. These are collected in section v.

Section vi, -A-B, of course begs the question, since it takes for granted that we do have subdivisions, but that some of these subdivisions are demarcated solely by the cogency and coherence of their neighbors, themselves conforming to neither of the established criteria. Obviously, we cannot claim that such a conglomerate constitutes a subdivision deliberately formed within redactional processes, for the absence of positive criteria prevents it. All we are able to do is take note of the presence, among many subdivisions which clearly have been put together in accord with noteworthy internal criteria, of a few aggregations of two or more cognitive units lacking any internal traits of deliberate agglutination.

We cannot ignore signs of the division of originally coherent subdivisions, e.g., presently separated cognitive units which conform to a single, internally-unitary formulary patterns, and which deal with a cogent, even narrowly defined, theme. Such units are catalogued in section vii.

Finally, in section viii, we ask whether the intermediate divisions as a whole yield any further evidence of a deliberate redactional program for their segregation, aggregation and internal construction.

ii. Intermediate Divisions Defined by both Internally-unitary Formulary Traits and Coherent Themes

We here catalogue the most interesting kind of intermediate division of our order, that which exhibits both a coherent theme and a highly disciplined, internally-unitary mode of articulation or formulation. Here there can be no doubt of the coincidence of redaction and formulation.

Kelim

1. 1:1-9: The chapter consists of two matched catalogues, each containing twenty entries, 1:1-4 and 1:5-9. The point is to contrast uncleanness with holiness. The theme is degrees of uncleanness (1:1-4, 1:5) as against degrees of holiness (1:6-9).

2. 10:1-2: The unit consists of two lists, 10:1A: These utensils afford protection with ... + 10 items + explanatory matter. 10:2: With what do they stop up?

3. 17:1-3, 4-12: These two groups are tightly organized in form and theme. 17:1-3 follow: X -- its measure is +B+substantive. The reason I treat this set as integral to the principal group, 17:4-12, is that the latter takes up the definition of 17:1's pomegranates, and then repeats the matter, 17:5. Pomegranate of which they have spoken, 17:6, egg, 17:7, fig, etc. This set is somewhat complex and certainly is not so smooth as ordinary lists. But the internally unitary formulary traits of 17:5A, 6A, 7A, 8A, C, E, 9A must be taken into account. 17:11-12 are internally disciplined as well. In any event the inner coherence of the whole, both in formulation and in theme, is striking. I count the following units: 17:1A, C, D, E, 2A, 3A=6; 17:5A, 6A, 7A, 8A, C, E, 9A=7; 17:11A, D, 12A=3.

4. 21:1-3: The pronounced formal-redactional trait is he who touches (sometimes understood) + list + unclean/clean, so 21:1A, B, C, D, 2A, B, C, and 3A, B, C - 10 in all, certainly a unitary construction. 21:1D violates the list-form in its predicate. The common theme is parts of the loom, wagon, and other wooden objects.

5. 24:1-15 + 16-17: The shared formulary traits obviously are internal to the formulation of each entry. There are three..., X is subject to midras, Y to corpse-uncleanness, Z is clean of all, 24:1, 2, 3, 4, 5, 6, 7, 8, 9, 10, 11, 12, 13, 14, 15. 24:16 slightly changes the internal formulation, and 24:17 treats the formulary as external to its materials, drawing only on the opening clause. Accordingly, fundamental are fifteen entries. The common theme is the difference between midras - corpse-uncleanness.

6. 29:1-8: Lists on the common theme of extensions of an object deemed connected to the principal object join internal form to theme. 29:1A-B, C, D-E, 3A, B, C, 4A, B -- all list items, then a predicate consisting of an ordinal number. The next group, 29:5A-D -- (one) handbreadth; 29:6A-D, two; 6E, three; 29:7A, B, four; 29:7C, D, five; E, F, G, six; 29:8A, B-C, seven; 8D, eight; E + F, nine; E + G, ten. The ordinal pattern thus is internal to the formulation of the rule. There would seem to be 18 principal entries.

Ohalot

7. 1:1-3 + 4 (+5): The formulaic pattern of 1:1A-C, two, three, four, then is spelled out in the glosses, 1:1D, E, 1:2-3F (+6). The theme is corpse-uncleanness and its effects. The secondary development of the primary formulaic pattern is at 1:4, carried out at 1:5 as well but now with a shift in subject-matter. 1:6 clearly commences a new subdivision.

8. 8:1-5 (+6): There are things which bring uncleanness and interpose, bring and do not interpose, interpose and do not bring, do not interpose and do not bring + These (8:1B, 3A, 4A, 5A). The unity of form and theme is obvious. 8:6 is appended.

9. 9:1-14 (+15, 16): The theme is the hive. The form is apocopation. The units are internally closely matched against one another, in a series of perfect correspondences. 9:15-16 are appended due to common theme. The units are 9:1-2, 9:3-4, 9:5-6, 9:7-8, 9:9, 9:10, 9:11-12, 9:13, 9:14 -- 9 in all.

10. 10:1-7: This sizable unit, on the corpse-matter and the hatchway, consists of closely balanced apocopated sentences at 10:1-2, 4, 5, 6, and 7, then disputes phrased in

apocopation for the apodosis as well as the protasis, 10:3. The principal entries are 10:1, 2, 3, 4, 5, 6-7 -- 6 in all.

11: 13:5-6: These diminish the handbreadth +10; these do not diminish +10 + glosses. The form and theme are inextricable.

Negaim

12. 3:3-8: This summary-construction is formulated in extremely tight repetitive form, a declarative sentence followed by distinct illustrative clauses in apposition (not apocopation), five entries in all, balanced clause by clause. The group introduces each principal theme of tractate, Chapters Four through Thirteen. At the head of the tractate, it would have been deemed a proem.

Parah

13. 11:4-6: The sentences are closely balanced against one another in every possible way. The theme is the differentiation between uncleanness decreed in the Torah and that decreed by the scribes. There are three base-units.

14. 12:6F, 7-8D: The theme is the absence of counting removes in purification-rites, stated by 12:6E, then with closely matched sets, 12:7, 12:8A-D -- 3 in all.

Tohorot

15. 1:5-6: This sizable unit begins in a generalization, stated as a fully articulated sentence, A, +how so? Then we have closely balanced, apocopated sentences, B, C, D, E, F, G, 1:6A, B, C, D, E, F, G (declarative sentence), H, I. J, K, L,M -- 20 entries in all. The theme is mixtures of food in several removes of uncleanness.

16. 1:7-9 (+2:1): The whole group is heavily apocopated, in the following stichs: 1:7A-D, +E, F-G, H-I, 1:8A-B, C-D, E-F, 1:9A-B, C, D -- 9 stichs, in groups of 3. The common theme is removes of uncleanness and disconnection, as at M. Kel. 18:5, etc. 2:1 carries the same theme forward, also the form, apocopation, but is no longer balanced, clause by clause, with 1:9. However, it persists in the pattern of internally fairly well balanced stichs, clause by clause. Its units are 2:1A-C, D-E, F, G, H-J, K, L1, L2 (and she saw), M1, M2, N -- 11 in all, (possibly) 20 for the whole.

17. 2:3-7 (+ 2:2, 2:8): 2:3-7, which deal with degrees of sanctification and their susceptibility to uncleanness in various removes, are exquisitely balanced at 2:3-5, 9 stichs, repeated at 2:6, then 2:7 goes over the same matter with 3 entries, each of 3 stichs, all of them articulated within a single highly disciplined pattern. 2:2, a well balanced dispute, introduces the whole, and 2:8 is a miscellaneous item, joined at the end for its thematic, but not formal, congruity.

18-20. See iii 70.

Miqvaot

21. 1:1B-I, 1:2, 1:3, 1:4-5, matched item for item at 1:6B-L (+1:4T-Y, 1:5): The common theme is the contrast between water in ponds, 1:1B, and rain-drippings which

have not ceased, 1:6B. Each item is stated as a complete sentence, with if understood, 9 against 9, 18 in all, and a single formulary pattern governs the whole subdivision. 1:4T-Y glosses, and 1:5 is an inserted Houses' dispute.

Niddah

22. 5:3-5, 6: This set on the rules applicable to several age-groups is formulated in closely-balanced declarative sentences, 5:3C-L + M = 5:5A-H = 5:4A-H + I. See Part XV, pp. 81-86. 5:6 is carefully balanced internally, 5:6A-C = D-F, G = H, syllable by syllable.

Makhshirin: None

Zabim

23. See iii 1-2. 5:1, 2, and 3-4 can be seen as three separate subdivisions, with internally unitary formulary patterns as well as distinctive organizing or thematic traits.

24. 5:6-10 + 11, 23: The persistent internal formulary pattern is he who + verbs + predicate + imparts uncleanness, etc., + [if] he separated, he imparts. The theme, transfer of uncleanness of diverse sources by diverse modes, is worked out in the following units: 5:6, 5:7, 5:8A-B, C-D, 5:9 -- 5 principal entries, expanded at 5:10A, B-D. To the set are appended 2 independent items, 5:11 and the catalogue of things which make heave-offering unfit. 5:12B, C, D; E-F, G -- 3 items, and H -- 2 items, 10 in all.

Tebul Yom: None

Yadayim: None

Uqsin: None

Nos. 2, 4, and 8 may belong in section iii, since they are little more than well-constructed lists. The specific entries on the lists, however, do seem to follow a single formulary pattern, and, in the balance, they seem better situated in the present catalogue.

In all, I count 20 subdivisions which exhibit both coherent themes and internally-unitary formulary patterns, exclusive of 4 cross-references. Of these, the following stand at the commencement or conclusion of principal divisions: Nos. 1, 7, 15-16, 21, 24, to which should be added No. 12, which introduces the immense unit on the bright of Negaim, 7 in all, or 35% of the whole.

The following constitute successive sequences of subdivisions organized within the stated criteria: Nos. 8, 9, 10; 17 continuing Nos. 15-16, which themselves may be regarded as a single entry; 23-24, 25% of the whole (exclusive of No. 23, which is a cross-referenced item). It therefore appears that there is a process of double-redaction before us, formation of a subdivision along the lines of the stated criteria, then its agglutination with still another subdivision formed on the same lines.

Those intermediate divisions which serve to begin or end principal divisions obviously are the work of ultimate redaction, and the same is to be said of those which constitute by themselves major corpora of cognitive units, 60% of the whole. In these cases the work of the tradent and that of the redactor indubitably coincide.

Nos. 2, 3, 4, and 6 -- 20% -- do not exhibit quite the same rigid discipline of formulation of cognitive units as the others. The following subdivisions both exhibit very tight formal and thematic organization and effect no readily-discerned, larger redactional purpose: Nos. 5, 13, 14, and 22 -- 20% of the whole. It seems fair to conclude that the stated criteria are applied chiefly in the work of th ultimate organization and redaction of the principal divisions, and only to a much diminished extent in the work of the agglutination of intermediate divisions. When people got to work on the organization of tractates, they will have had in hand already-formed aggregates of cognitive units (those in section iii), and to these they added, commonly to mark the beginning or the end of a principal division, intermediate divisions which they themselves both formulated and constructed as aggregates. The significant exempla of the work are in our first list, Nos. 1, 7, 12, 15-16, 21, 24. Those entries which form successive exempla of subdivisions shaped in accord with a single formulary and thematic program, Nos. 8-10, 15-17, and 23-24, clearly suggest a second redactional function, which was to form units smaller than the principal divisions but larger than the various and diverse intermediate divisions. If that was the intent, little seems to have been done to realize it.

What do Nos. 5, 13, 14, and 22 have in common? No. 5 is the work of Judah, giving repetitious illustration to his conceptions (Part II, pp. 22-23). No. 13 certainly is the work of tradents in the circle of Meir; the pericope is clear on that matter. No. 14 simply repeats the same thing in the same pattern three times. No. 22 is important and exceptional. Accordingly, while the stated pattern was utilized in the work of ultimate redactors, it obviously was not their invention. It was utilized by tradents of two identifiable circles of Usha for the formation of sizable units -- intermediate divisions -- of materials on a single theme by a single master (or, in Meir's instance, by his opposition, "sages"). But it does not seem to have been much used, and its aesthetic promise was realized primarily by the redactors at work on the last stages in the formation of principal divisions. Before us is a tradental form, that is, a form serviceable, even though autonomous of large-scale redaction, in the organization of a given authority's materials and their linguistic formalization. Such formed materials come to serve a clearcut redactional function in the later states of the organization of an intermediate division of the order. The absence of named authorities in this last phase in the utilization of the form certainly conforms to the purposes and plans of the ultimate redactors.

iii. _Intermediate Divisions Defined by both Externally-Unitary Formulary Traits and Coherent Themes_

The sizable catalogue before us includes 125 of the 171 intermediate divisions of our Order, 75% of the whole:

ii	20	12%
iii	125	75%
iv	13	8%
v	5	3%
vi	4	2%
		100%

If we treat together the two types of formulary traits internally-unitary and externally-unitary, we see that 87% of the subdivisions exhibit striking correlations of formal distinctiveness and thematic coherence. The importance of formulary coherence is seen when we add to that figure the 3% of subdivisions shaped around common forms without a common theme, 90% of the whole. It follows that the normal policy in the delineation of intermediate divisions is to state the constituent primary cognitive units in such a way as to impose upon their formulary construction some indication of a distinctive formal character.

Let us now proceed to catalogue the largest and definitive group of intermediate divisions. We here pay close attention to the number of cognitive units of which each subdivision is composed. It is to be stressed that the enumerative analysis of the intermediate divisions into their cognitive units is not so precise. To the best of my ability, I have applied a single criterion throughout, namely, the recognition that the result of a single uninterrupted process of thought on a single issue, theme, or problem is before us. But that criterion is not so exactly to be applied as those by which we have distinguished one intermediate division from another. That is why in many instances the number of cognitive units specified for an intermediate division should be seen as, at best, an estimate. With equally good and sound reason others may readily discern a different number of distinct units in a given subdivision. I also stress that the common formulary or formal pattern specified for a fair number of intermediate divisions is, simply, declarative sentences. While these are spelled out, the analysis of the types and forms of declarative sentences will be undertaken in Chapter Three. Many intermediate divisions turn out to be formed of rigidly patterned declarative sentences.

Kelim

1. 2:2-8: This set has a formulary superstructure and substructure. Its major formulary pattern is a catalogue, The ... which are among clay utensils, 2:2A: Smallest; 2:3A: clean; 2:7: unclean.

Each catalogue's heading is then followed by a list, 2:2A1-C; 2:3B-H: 2:7B-C -- 3. The formulary substructure is the pattern: x unclean/y clean, at 2:4A, B, C (+ glosses in dispute form); 2:5A, B, (+ glosses in dispute form); 2:6A-C (+ dispute [and see 5:5, below, No. 6]. 2:7D-G, H-J and 2:8 diverge from the pattern and are joined only by theme. The common theme of the unit is whether or not diverse clay objects are susceptible.

2. 3:1-2: This set is formulated in declarative sentences, around the key-word S'WR. The common theme is the measure of a break in a clay utensil which renders said utensil useless. The formulary unity is not pronounced. The units are 3:1B, C, D; 3:2A-C, D-E, F, G, H, I-K -- 9.

3. 3:3-4, 6-8 (+ 3:5): What formally unites this set of five units is noun + S + tightly joined predicate, plus 3:3: A jar which was perforated ..., if in the place of ...is ...; 3:4: A jar which cracked ... even though ..., is clean. The pattern shifts to the duplicated subject at 3:6: scutchgrass with which they line .. -- that which touches ...; 3:7 a kettle which ... -- that which touches ...; 3:8: A jar which ... -- that which touches ....3:5 breaks the pattern for the protasis -- one who touches -- but preserves the apocopation of of the apodosis. The common theme is the repair of clay utensils; a subdominant theme is connection of the material used for repair to the primary utensil.

4. 4:1-2, 4:3C-D, E-G, 4A-D (+ 4:3A-B): The pattern is noun + S + apodosis tightly linked to protasis -- thus, complex declarative sentences, 4:1: a sherd which ... is clean + dispute at B-C, D, which yield a jar which ... is unclean/clean, just as at A; 4:2: a jar which ... is clean; a spoiled jar which ... is clean, because ...; 4:4: a clay utensil which ... if ... all are clean/unclean; if ... unclean/clean. 4:3A-B gloss 4:2: what is a spoiled jar? Then, 4:3C-D: [a jar] in which were ... any part which ... receives, any part which ... receives ... 4:3E-G follow suit. The common theme of the unit is clay jar and other utensils -- entries.

5. 4:4E, 5:1-2 + 3: The superstructure is, X -- when does it receive uncleanness? + gloss. Thus 4:4E: clay utensils, when do they receive ...? When ... and it is the completion ... 5:5A + E: A baking oven ... when ... and when is ...? 5:2A, D-D: A double-stove ... when is ...? The substructure is formed of the tightly formulated disputes, 5:1B-E, matched at 5:2B. The set then is augmented at M. 5:2F-K, 5:3, with materials joined by the common theme, attachments to the oven. While phrased in disciplined forms, these elements do not exhibit closely matching recurrent patterns. The common theme, of course, is ovens. There are 3 primary entries, 4:4E/A, 5:1, 5:2A-D.

6. 5:4A [-- 5:5], 6, 7, (+ 8), 9 (+ 10) + 11: The fundamental stylistic unity is imposed by noun + S + verb, etc., specifically, an oven which. 5:8 and 5:10 continue 5:7 and 5:9, respectively, with [if] one divided it. 5:4A is supplemented by a ma^{C}aseh (5:4B). 5:5 is formally out of phase (x/clean/y unclean + reason) and belongs with 2:4-6. In theme and pattern, however, it fits with 5:3. 5:11 gives us our noun S (oven which), but this is not followed by an active verb. Rather we have a variation on x/unclean, y/clean; then [if] it was ... Perhaps we should have been better served by oven [which is of stone or metal], [supply which (S)] was perforated, damaged, cracked ..., with a suitable apodosis. Then the opening proposition, 5:11A, is inserted and spoils (established) redactional formulary preferences. In any event, 5:11 certainly is thematically quite in place.

7. 6:1-4: This certainly forms a formally coherent chapter, since the basic units entirely are in apocopation, 6:1A-B, C-D, E + F (dispute), G-H, 5:2A-D, E-F, H-J, 6:3A-D (+ E-M), 6:4A-C, D-E. the common theme is makeshift stoves. There can be no doubt as to the shift in theme both fore (5:11) and aft (7:1). Nonetheless, the sort of inter-nally-unitary formulary traits which locate a set in list ii are not constituted by the clauses here, which do not pretend to balance one another. I count 10 entries.

8. 7:1-5: This group is in simple declarative sentences, 7:1: A fire-basket which ... is unclean, for ..., [if] ..., it is clean. [If] one ... it is clean, etc. 7:2 follows suite +

dispute, D-E, either stich of which yields an acceptable conclusion to 7:2D. 7:3 is exactly parallel to 7:2. 7:4-5 begin with an understood if. Sentences include a less/more sequence, 7:1C, 7:3E, 7:4C, E, 7:5E -- 5. The common theme is parts of the oven. The basic entries are 7:1A-B, 7:2A, 7:3A-B + C, 7:4A-C, 7:5A.

9. 8:1-8, 10-11 (+ 8:9), 9:1 (+ 2), 3-7C (+ 9:7D-J, 8): The intermediate division is characterized by apocopation, e.g., is unclean; + 8:1D-F, G-J (dispute + debate), etc. Brief clauses, set off from one another, mark the whole. 8:9 is formally separate, as is 9:2, which is a Houses' dispute, stated in complete sentences. Yet 9:2A, if completed by B, is lightly apocopated in that the apodosis, B, refers not to the jar, the subject of A, but to elements of the predicate of the protasis. The apocopation of the remainder is marked, down to 9:7. The rest of 9:7 and 9:8 is a set of disputes completing 9:7A-C. The whole deals with the contamination of ovens, except for 8:9, which does not belong, and 9:2, which deals with a jar in the tent of a corpse. Neither the formulary pattern nor the theme shifts from 8:11 to 9:1, but 10:1 clearly inaugurates a new unit. The units are 8:1A-C, D-F, G-H, 8:2A-C (+ D-L), 8:3A-E, F-J; 8:4, 8:5A-D, E-H, 8:6, 8:7 (+ 8), 8:10A-E, 8:11, 9:1A-C, 9:2A, 9:3A-C, D-F, 9:4, 9:5, 9:6, 9:7A-C -- 21 in all.

10. 10:3-8: Apart from the opening segment 10:3A-C, we have apocopation, 10:3A-C, D-F, G-H, 10:4A-B + C, D, E; 10:5; 10:6A-B (the subject of A is not the subject of B); 10:6C-F, G-L, 10:7A-D, E-F, 10:8A-E, F + G-N -- 12 in all. Deleting words supplied in square brackets shows the full extent of the apocopation affecting the whole set. The theme is uncleanness imparted to clay utensils in the Tent and its prevention by a tight seal -- which theme is shared with 10:1-2 (ii2).

11. 11:2-3 + 4-9, 12:1-8, 13:1: The first two items are lists, Every ... is unclean except + 7 items; He who makes utensils from + 10 items ... clean (= mild apocopation). The remaining entries share a formulary preference for x/unclean, y/clean, 11:3D + F + H; 11:4A-B, F-G; 11:5A, 11:6A-B + D, E-F + I; 11:7A-B, C + E-F, H, 11:8A, 12:1A-B, C-D, E-F, H; 12:2C, D, E, F, G, H; 12:3A + C-D, F, G; 12:4A, C + F-G; 12:5A-B, C-D, + F -- certainly the dominant, if not exclusive, pattern. The theme is unclean and clean metal objects. I count 27 exempla.

12. 13:2-4B, + 5B: X which lost its y is unclean because of its z. If its z was removed, it is unclean because of its y -- 13:2A-B, C, D, E, 13:3B, 13:4A. The theme is metal utensils -- 6 entries.

13. 13:4-C-5: A saw one of every of whose teeth is removed is clean. If there remain ..., ... unclean. The same pattern is at 13:4C, as given, D-E, 13:5A, D, E -- 5 in all. The theme is as stated.

14. 13:6-8: This set exhibits a mild preference for x/unclean, y/clean, 13:6A, D, 13:8A-B, C/D (clean, clean vs. unclean, unclean). 13:7 sets forth simple but smooth declarative sentences, in matched pairs, A and B. It is difficult to claim that a single pattern is predominant, but the several units clearly are patterned. The theme is the relationship, as to uncleanness, of wood and metal, as announced at 13:6A. That statement certainly justifies testing the set as a unit.

15. 15:1F-S, 2-4B: 15:1F-K are matched, line by line, by L-R. Both form long declarative sentences, laden with qualifying materials, all smoothly joined from the subject, through the subordinate clauses, to the predicate. 15:2A depends upon unclean/clean + unclean (B), likewise 15:2F, G-H, I-J, 15:3A (+ B-C). 15:4 reverts to the sizable sentences of 15:1, All ... are unclean, except ..., All ... clean, except ..., a neat union of the two formulary patterns, the major declarative sentence of 15:1 and unclean/clean of 15:2-3. I think that the paramount pattern must be unclean/clean, which, after all, serves 15:1F-S. If so, we have the following exempla: 15:1F-K/L-R (+ 1), 2A, F, G-H, I-J, A, 3A, 4A-B -- 8 in all. There also are disputes, 15:1F-S, 2C-E, H-I, 15:3, 15:4A-B -- 5.

16. 15:4C, 5 (+ 6), 16:1A-B: This is the general rule (15:4C, 5B) + illustrative materials. 15:6 is made up of unclean/clean sequences, A, B, C-D, F. The theme is wooden objects at 15:4-5.

17. 16:1C-F, 2-4: X -- from what time does it receive uncleanness, 16:1C + D, F (wood), 16:2A, B, C, D; 3A, B, C, D, E (wooden baskets), 16:4A-B, D, F, H (leather utensils) -- 15 entries.

18. 16:5-8: The next set takes up baskets (16:5), then leather objects -- gloves, bags, covers, sheathes (16:6-8). The predominant form is the list or catalogue, 16:7-8, and unclean/clean, 16:5-6. I think the group is set where it is because it expands 16:1-4. The whole group -- 16:1C-8 -- probably should be treated as a secondary redactional development out of two primary groups which exhibit unitary formulary traits. Unclean/clean predominate at 16:5A, D-D, 16:6A-B, 16:7D, 16:8F-H, L -- 6 entries.

19. 18:4-7 (+ 8)-9: The formulary trait uniting this group, but external to the fundamental internal forms or patterns of the several units, is the use of noun + S + verb, 18:4: bed-frame which one set; 18:5: bed which was; 18:6: bed which was; 18:7: leg which was; 18:9: bed which was -- 5 in all. (The one unit which violates the form, 18:8, also deals with a different object, a phylactery; its principle, however, is identical to the foregoing.) The theme and principle are the bed and its uncleanness when whole and when dismantled.

20. 19:5-20:7: The common external formal trait of this sizable set is noun + S + verb, at 19:5A, 19:6A, [19:7A (was understood)], 19:8A, 19:9A, 19:10A, 20:1A, 20:2E, 20:3A, 20:4A, 20:5A, 20:6A, 20:7A -- 12 units. The pattern decisively shifts at 21:1. A further common formulary trait is the development of the idea of the pericope in long declarative sentences, 19:5-6, 7, 20:1, 20:3, 5. Disputes mark the others; either stich of the apodosis completes the protasis as a declarative sentence. The theme of the whole is the shift in the status as to uncleanness of an object whose component parts are revised or removed, or -- parallel to this -- whose basic character is altered, e.g., by damage, or by adaptation to some purpose other than the principal one. 20:2A-D, which breaks the formal pattern, also is uninterested in the primary problem and principle, being concerned with whether an object is susceptible to midras or corpse-uncleanness. It serves as prologue to 20:2E-G, which follow the established form and treat the prevailing theme.

21. 22:1-10, 23:1: As at No. 20, the dominant redactional-formulary trait is noun + S + verb, 22:1A, 2A, 3A, C, 4A, E, 5A, 6A, 7A, 8A, 9A, D, 10F, 23:1A, D -- 15 in all. 23:1D introduces 23:3-4's subject, but the thematic problem of that group is different (see v 4). The common theme is the same principle as is expressed in the same redactional formulary at No. 20, namely, the affect of adaptation or damage upon the susceptibility of an object, e.g., to corpse or midras-uncleanness. This theme pertains also to 22:10, even though the form at A-E diverges from the established one. But 22:9D-E's form is continued at 22:10A-E, so the proper division of pericopae is clear. If 22:10 began at F, it would fit into the larger construction. Perhaps 19:5-20:7 and 22:1-23:1 should be seen as a single massive intermediate division, consisting of 25 pericopae. Chapter Twenty-four follows with 15 -- 40 in all, or a "tractate" of about 5 chapters.

22. 25:1-9: The common redactional form is noun(s) + have insides and outside, 25:1A (C,D), 2A, B, 3A, 7A, 9A -- 6 in all. 7B-8 develop 7A. 25:4-5 are joined by the stated theme to the larger structure, dealing with the quarter-measure. 25:6C explicitly depends upon the redactional formulary. There is no doubt that the whole forms an intermediate division, even though the salient redactional-thematic formulary does not predominate in each entry.

23. 27:1-2: We have a descending ordinal sequence, 5-1, then an ascending one, 1-5. The common theme is susceptibility of diverse materials. The common formulary traits are external, since 27:1A-E do not generate equivalently succinct entries, but are glossed. 27:3-4 are essential to the foregoing, but diverge in form. See also v 6.

24. 27:3-4: He who makes ... -- it is unclean. He who cuts ..., etc. The theme is mixtures of materials and segments of materials. The pattern of mild apocopation is at 27:3A, understood at D, 27:4A, understood at C, and G-5.

25. 28:5-6: The common theme is changes in status as to uncleanness accompanying changes in the character of a fabric. The common form is long and well disciplined declarative sentences, 27:5A + B or C + D, E, 27:5F + G, or H + I -- 3 sentences.

Ohalot

26. 1:6-8, 2:1 (+ 2), 3-5 (+ 3:3F-G, 4-5): The common theme is the point at which man imparts corpse-uncleanness and the parts of the man which do so. The formulary pattern is simple declarative sentences, which tend at 1:7B and 1:8A to form catalogues. The materials of 2:1-5 exhibit the same trait still more pronouncedly; 2:1A: These contaminate through overshadowing; 2:3: These contaminate through contact and carriage but not overshadowing (+ 2:4: The rolling stone, etc., contaminate through contact + overshadowing but not carriage), 2:5: These if lacking are clean. 2:2A-B are formally and thematically out of place. The issue is located here because it supplements 2:1's list. Treating 1:6-8 and 2:1 (+ 2), 3-5 as a simple subdivision seems justified by the coherent there and the general form, even though 2:1ff. comprise a clearcut subunit of the whole. 3:3F-G, 4-5 complete this set, reverting back to both its theme and its form at 3:3F-G. 3:4 shifts to apocopation to illustrate 3:3F-G, and 3:5 alludes to 2:2A, mixed blood, These are cut off by the intervening unit, below, No. 27. I count the following sentences: 1:6A-B, D, D-E, 1:7; 1:8A, B-C, which leads into 2:1, 3A, 4A, 5A -- 10.

27. 2:6-7, 3:1-2 (+ 3A-E): The form is disputes, 2:6, 2:7A-C (+D), E-G, H-J, 3:1A-C, D-L, 3:2A-C. But these yield simple sentences. 3:2D-G shifts to declarative sentences, continued at 3:3A-E -- 9 sentences in all. The common theme is corpse-matter or an analogous substance which is divided but under a single roof. The materials of 3:2D-G and 3:3A-E are not on the same theme, but are appended because they relate to the affect of the roof of the house on contaminants scattered under it. 3:2D-3:3E form a unit unto themselves, but their location is explicable and deliberate.

28. 3:6-7, 4:1-3: The form is a declarative sentence + extended illustrations in apocopation. 3:6 introduces the whole; 3:7A presents a generalization, B-I, J-P, Q-U forming three sets of apocopated sentences in illustration thereof. The topic is passage of uncleanness through a cubic handbreadth. Apocopation is at 4:1A-F, G-L, 4:2A-G, 4:3A-F, G-I. In all -- 3, then 5.

29. 5:1-4: The form is mild apocopation yielded by Houses' disputes, 3 in all, which spin out the theme of overshadowing, with particular reference to apertures and protrusions. The units are 5:1A + B or C, 5:2A + B or C or D, 5:3A + B or C (simple sentence, if understood). 5:4 again yields apocopation. A-B + C, D-E + F, perfectly matched. Still, the base unit of enumeration here appears to be 3 -- that is, the Houses' disputes.

30. 5:5-7, 6:1-7, 7:1-2: The dominant form is a generalization stated as a declarative sentence, followed by heavily apocopated illustrations. The overall theme is interposition and overshadowing, 5:5: Joining a utensil to the wall of a tent + 5:7B-K; 6:1A, man and utensils are tents for contamination but not purification + 6:1B-F, 6:2A, B, C; 6:3, a wall which ... is judged + 6:3B-F, 6:4, 5; 6:6A, a house which ... is judged + 6:6B-F + 6:7; 7:1, apocopation lacking a generalization; 7:2A: all sloping sides of Tents ... + 7:2B-H. The generalizations are 5:5C, D1, 2, 3, 5:6E, 5:7A, 6:1A, 6:2A, B, C, 6:3A, 6:4A, 6:6, 5:5A, 6:7A, 7:1A-B, C, D, E, F; 7:2A -- evidently 21 in all.

31. 7:3-6: One common form is disputes, 7:3A-D + E-F, 7:4A-C, 7:5A-B, 7:6 is appended, joined by a common theme. A second formulary trait is the simple sentence with if understood, at 7:3A, B, C, E, 7:5A, B -- 6. 7:4A and 7:5A are matched in mild apocopation. The theme is the corpse in the house, unfolding through distinct issues, 7:3, opening affected by the corpse; 7:4, the woman who dies in labor; 7:5, the stillborn child. The common theme is thus expressed through disciplined, but diverse patterns.

32. 11:1-6 (+ 7), 8: The formally unitary traits are, first, Houses' disputes, which, second, are phrased in declarative sentences, with if understood, specifically, 11:1B, 11:3, 11:4, 11:5, 11:6 -- five in all. 11:2 is in apocopation; it is integral to the unfolding of the theme, the way in which uncleanness is transmitted by living creatures, 11:2-6. 11:7 is appended because its issue is dependent on the foregoing. 11:8 follows the form, an apocopated Houses' dispute. But its issue is that of No. 33.

33. 11:9, 12:1-7 (+ 8): The form is pure apocopation. Each item commences noun + S + verb, 11:9A, 12:1A, 12:2A, 12:3A, 12:4A, 12:5A, 12:6A, 12:7A, but not at 12:8. The theme shifts as at 11:8, from a living creature to a utensil's affects in overshadowing or interposing, (as at 6:1ff.) 12:8 is discrete, a dispute, not apocopated, on the affect of the

lintel. The theme is what joins the unit to its larger setting. Apocopation is at 11:9V, C, 12:1, B, D, 2A, C, 3A (+ B-C), 4A, 5A, D, 6A -- evidently 12 entries.

34. 13:1-4: After the he who makes opening, 13:1A the primary formulary pattern, uniting the sequence, 13:1-3, is x its measure is ..., understood at B, explicit at 13:1A, D, E, F, 13:2A, B, C, 13:3A + dispute, D -- 10 in all. 13:4 starts he who makes and then rehearses the form. The theme is apertures through which uncleanness passes.

35. 14:1-3: The form is substantial declarative sentences, 14:1A + D, E, 14:2A, B, 14:3A -- 5 in all. The theme is the wall-projection as a Tent.

36. 14:4-7: The theme is a wall-projection as a Tent, but the form is severe apocopation, characterizing the inserted disputes. Perhaps, as above, we should treat the declarative sentences of No. 35 as integral to the illustrative materials of No. 36. The units are 14:4, 5A-D, E, F-G, 14:6, 14:7 -- 6 in all (?).

37. 15:1-7: 15:1 is a set of declarative sentences, followed, at 15:2A + 3, 4, 5, 6, 7, by a series of apocopated cases illustrative of the affects of overshadowing by solid objects, 6 in all. 15:4-7 deal with a divided house, all in apocopation. Declarative sentences are at 15:A, B-C, 15:2C -- 3, 9 all together.

38. 15:8-10: Each clause depends upon a he who ... it is ... -- apocopation -- construction, often with the apodosis given before the protasis constituted by he who, thus, 15:8A, the forecourt ..., he who stands ..., 15:9A: a jar which is ..., he who touches; 15:9B, a cow which ... he who touches -- 3 in all. 15:10A, B then return to the natural order, he who touches ..., they are unclean -- ten all together.

39. See v 10.

40. 16:2F-I, 16:3-5, 17:1-5, 18:1-10: This vast unit deals with areas in which corpses are found, grave-areas, and rules pertaining to them. All the subunits are simple declarative statements, of various kinds to be sure, 16:2F, G, H, I; 16:3A (2x), B, C, D-E, 16:4A, B, C, 16:5A, B (3x), C, 17:1A, B + C, D + E, 17:2A, B, C (3x); 17:3, 17:4, 17:5A-C, D + E, F; 18:1A + B, C + D; 18:2A, B (slight apocopation), C-E, F, G; 18:3A, B, C; 18:4A, B, C, D; 18:5A-C + D, E-F; 18:6A, B, C; 18:7A, B, C + D; 18:8A-C, 18:9A, B, C, D; 18:10 -- something like 60 simple sentences, in sequence.

Negaim

41. 1:1-3:2: While this sizable group exhibits formal subdivisions, in fact a single formulary trait, simple declarative sentences, characterizes a single thematic unit, unclean plagues, their colors, effects, examination. There are, to be sure, disputes, e.g., 1:1C-D, 1:2, 1:4, 2:2E-G, but these always yield declarative sentences when the protasis is joined to one stich of the apodosis. And some of the disputes are, in fact, artificial. Apocopation is superficial, i.e., long sets of brief phrases, all of them completed by a single apodosis or serving to complete a single protasis, as at 1:3, 1:5-6. The principal complete declarative sentences are as follows: 1:1A-B + C or D; 1:2A or B; 1:3A-I, J; 1:4A or B or C, D, E, F, 1:5-6, 2:1A, B, C, D-F, 2:2A-D, E + F or G; 2:3A, B; 2:4A-F + G, H; 2:5A, B, C-D, E; 3:1A, B, C, D, E, F, G -- evidently 30 distinct entries.

42. 4:1-3: This unitary construction compares the traits of white hair, spreading, and quick flesh, 3 entries for 5 units, 4 for the last. The individual entries are not so tightly balanced as to warrant entry alongside 3:3-8 (ii 12), for some lack verbs and are simply continuations of declarative sentences.

43. 4:4-11: The whole is a sequence of apocopated units, 4:4A-E + F-H + I, then the bright-spot sequence, 4:4J-M, 4:5A-D, E-H, 4:6A-H, I-R; 4:7A-G, H-N; 4:8A-E, 4:9A-E; F-J; 4:10A-F, G-K, L-P, Q-V; 4:11A-E (+ F-H). the key word, bright-spot, joins 15 distinct but closely related entries. There is a fair number of disputes, always phrased in accord with the prevailing redactional-formulary preference. The common theme is the bright spot, of course. The reason the set belongs here and not at ii is the same as stated above, No. 42.

44. 5:1-6:6: The sustained formulary pattern is the declarative sentence followed by heavily apocopated examples, 5:1A-B (declarative sentence), C-H, 5:2A-F, G-L, M-R: 5:3A-C (dispute, A + B or A + C yield a sentence), D-F + G or H, I+J-M + N, 5:4A-C (declarative sentence), D-J + K, 5:5A (declarative sentence), B-F + G-I, 6:1 (declarative sentence), 6:2, 6:3, 6:4, 6:5A-E, F-H, 6:6 -- 5 declarative sentences, perhaps 15 apocopated units (depending on how these are divided; the matter is less clear). The overall theme is unclean plague marks. The subdivisions of the unit are marked by shifts in the treatment of the general theme, specifically 5:1-3, 5:4-5, 6:1-4 + 6:5-6, three in all.

45. 6:7-8,7:1: This set consists of three long lists, 6:7, twenty-four tips of limbs are not susceptible through quick flesh; 6:8, places not susceptible through a bright spot; 7:1, clean bright spots. The common theme is obvious. But the lists are diverse in internal form and not comparable to, e.g., M. Oh. 8:1.

46. See v 11.

47. 9:1-3: The theme is the boil and burning. The common formulary pattern is the declarative sentence, 9:1A, B-D, E-G, 9:2A, B, C, D, E, F, G; 9:3 (ma^{c}aseh) -- 10 sentences.

48. See v 12.

49. 10:10: This brief subdivision deals with scalp and forehead-baldness, in simple declarative sentences, A-B, C-E, F-G, H, I -- 5.

50. 11:1-12: The single theme is fabrics and their susceptibility to plagues. The unifying formulary preference is declarative sentences: 11:1A-B, C-D, E, F-J; 11:2A-B, D, D + E; 11:3A-C, D, E (dispute); 11:4A-C, D, E-H+I; 11:5A, B, C, D-F (dispute), G-H, I-K + L; 11:6A-B (if understood), C-D, E-I + J (he who ... [if] ... one burns -- mild apocopation); 11:7A-B (a garment which ... they spread -- mild apocopation) C-G (colloquy), H; 11:8A-B (dispute), C, D-G, H-I; 11:9A-G (one who ..., lo, the second -- mild apocopation), H-I, J (dispute); 11:10A-B, C, D, E, F-H; 11:11A-E, F-G (mild apocopation), H, I; 11:12A-B (mild apocopation), C, D-E, F -- 45(?). Despite the diversity of the construction of the declarative sentences, the pattern is unmistakable. It continues to the end of the tractate, marked by shifts only of theme.

51. 12:1-7, 13:11-12: The subdivision on plagues in houses is a mixture of various sorts of simple declarative sentences. The disputes do not predominate and in any case

yield declarative sentences: 12:1A, B, C-D, 2A-C, D, E, F, 3A-G, H; 12:4A-C, D-E, F, G, 12:5A-C, D-E, F, G, 12:6A-B, C-D, E-F, G, H, I-K, L, [12:1 (major list)], 13:2A-C, D, E-I; 13:3A-C, D-E, F-G, H-I, J + K; 13:4A, B, C; 13:5A-C, D-F; 13:6A-D, E; 13:7A-B, C-D, E, F, G; 13:8A, B, C, D; 13:9A-C, D, E-G; 13:10A-C, D-F + G; 13:11A-D, E-F; 13:12A-B, C, D, E -- evidently 60 in all, excluding 13:1.

52.   14:1-13: The subdivision on purifying the leper is dominated by simple declarative sentences, most of them smooth and fully articulated. There are disputes at 14:9E-G, 14:10H-O, 14:11, and Judah glosses 14:8, 9, and 12. I count 55 (!) discrete sentences: 14:1A-B, C, D, E, F-G, H; 14:2A, B, C, D, E, F; 14:3A, B, C, D, E-F, G-H, I; 14:4, 14:5A-C, D, E, F-G, H-I, J, K; 14:6A-C, D; 14:7A, B,; 14:8A, B, C-D, E, F, G; 14:9A, B, C, D, E-G; 14:10A, B, C, D, E, F-G, H, I-M, N-O; 14:11A + B or C; 14:12A, B, C, D-E. We return to the problem of iii 50-52 below, p. 104.

Parah

53.   1:1-3 (+ 4): The dominant form is the dispute. There is no pretense at constructing coherent sentences, e.g., protasis + one stich of the apodosis, and top-ic-sentences are omitted, producing severely inarticulate units of thought even where disputes are lacking. 1:4 is formally out of phase, but participates in the theme, the age at which various animals are suitable for sacrifice. Disputes are at 1:1A-C, 1:2A-C, and the unit at 1:1F-V -- 3 groups. On the other hand, if we supply the necessary language, we get a set of sentences as follows: 1:1A-B, A heifer [is to be] a year old, and a cow [is to be] two years old, so too, C; D, "Even one five years old [is suitable]"; E. The old one is suitable, but ...; F-K, L-R, S-Y form a triplet of matched colloquies; 1:2A, Bullocks [are to be] two years old, + C, D-F (which match 1:1D-E);1:3G, Lambs [are to be] one year old; H, And rams [are to be] two years old, + I; J, then K, L, M, are matched; + N, O (duplicated subject); and 1:4A-C + D are matched at 1:4E-G, clause by clause. Accord-ingly, we have a group of internally matched units, 1:1A-B, D, E -- 3; 1:1F-Y -- 3; 1:2A, C, D -- E; 1:3G, H (+ I), J + N, O -- 3; 1:3K-M -- 3, and1:4A-C vs. E-G + F -- 3 units, 2 balanced and joined by F. It seems to me not far-fetched to see the whole as a set of grouped declarative sentences, internally balanced, in sets of 3.

54.   2:1-5: The theme is the red cow used for the purification rite, and once more, the principal form is the dispute, excluding only 2:3D-E, which carry forward sages' position of 2:3A(-C). Here we do have better articulation in some of the declarative sentences. The disputes are at 2:1A-B, C-D, 2:2D-F, 2:3A-C, 2:4, 2:5A-B, C-F, J-K -- 8 in all. The simple declarative sentences are as follows: 2:1A + B, balanced at C + D, E-I, 2:2A, B, C, D + E, 2:3A + B-C, D: E/F + G (6 vs. 3 + generalization); 2:4H, I, J; 2:5A + B, C, D, E, F, G-K (if understood at G, H, I, then mild apocopation at J/K). There appear to be subgroups as specified, and 20 entries in all. There are better examples of stylistic formalization.

55.   3:1-11: Like M. Neg. 14:1ff., the unit on how the cow was slaughtered is expressed entirely in a narrative style, wholly in declarative sentences, nearly all of them brief, simple and fully articulated. There are some intruded disputes and glosses

(disputes: 3:1C-D, 3:4B-C, 3:5B-G, 3:9K, 3:11H; glosses: 3:2E, 3:3E, 3:7C, 3:9D-E [dispute in sense, gloss in form]). The sentence-units are 3:1A, B (C-E), 2A, B, C, D, 3A, C, D, E, F, G, 4A, 5A/G, 6, 7A-B, D, E, F, 8A, B, C, D, 9A, B-C (+ D-E), F, G, H, I, J, 10A, B, C, D-E, 11F, G, I, J, K, L-N -- 40 in all (?).

56. 4:1-4: The dominant formulary trait once more is declarative sentences, with a few secondary disputes. The sentences tend to be somewhat longer and more complex than in the foregoing entry. Disputes are appended at 4:1G (to A-E), H-I, J-K. Otherwise the sequence of declarative sentences is uninterrupted, 4:1A-F, H, I, L, M, 2A, B, C, D, 3A, B, C, D, 4A, B, C,-D + E, F, G, H, I -- 20 items.

57. 5:1-4: The declarative sentence continues in this subdivision on utensils used in the rite, but there is a distinctive trait to the sentence, the he-who (H) or that which (S), completed by a smoothly joined predicate, 5:1A (B, C), 5:2A (with B, C closely joined in simple if sentences), 5:3A-B + C-D + E (dispute), 5:4A-C (dispute) and D-E (dispute) -- 6 entries. 5:5-9 do not reveal the same formulary unity among their several entries, even though the theme is the same as that of 5:1-4.

58. 6:1-5: As above, the predominant formulary pattern is the declarative sentence, expressed as he who or that which, followed by an apocopated apodosis, and smooth if sentences, 6:1, 6:3-4, 6:5 -- 3 basic entries. 6:2 is a dispute, if ... + apocopated apodosis. The theme is drawing water.

59. 7:1-4: This set exhibits a pronounced and prevailing preference for apocopation to work out its theme of drawing water. The distinction of No. 59 from No. 58 is unmistakable, and the inner coherence of the formulary pattern -- he-who -- recurs at the head of each subunit, 7:1A, D, F, 7:2, 7:3A, D, F -- 7 stichs, + 7:4, apocopation without the expected he who says at 7:4A, B, C, and D.

60. 7:5-12, 8:1 (+ 2-3): The he-who -- formulary pattern continues, but the theme shifts to rules of, rather than cases about, drawing and transporting the water, 7:5A, 7:6A, 7:7A, 7:8A, E, 7:9A, 7:10A, 7:11A, 7:12A, 7:12C, 8:1A (8:2A, 8:3A). The set commencing at 8:2 carries forward the he-who construction of 8:2A and 8:3A, but clearly, 8:2 is meant to link the set to 8:1. It hardly inaugurates a further sequence of he-who's. In all, once the discussion of mixing and drawing water commences at 6:1, we have the following he-who subunits: 6:1A, 6:3A, 6:5A, 7:1A, D, F; 7:2, 7:3A, D, F; understood at 7:4A, B, C, D; 7:5A, D; 7:6, 7:7, 7:8A, 7:9, 7:10, 7:11, 7:12A, C; 8:1A -- 25 in all. It here is clear that he-who is a secondary redactional form, since it does not affect the formulation of the subunits aggregated thereby.

61. 8:8-11, 9:1-9: The unit on unsuitable water is composed of simple declarative sentences, some of them arranged as a dispute. 8:9-10 are closely matched. 8:11 is a mixture of various sorts of simple sentences. Disputes yield simple sentences. 9:6, 7 and 8-9 form sizable declarative sentences. I count the following sentence-units: 8:8A-B, C-D, E-F; 9A-C, D-F, G + H, I-J, K-L, M-N, O + P; 11R, S, T-U + V, W-X, 9:1A-C, D-F, H-I, 2A-D, E, F-G, 3A-B, C-D, E-F (+ G-H), 4A-C, D-H, 5A-C + D, E-F + G-H, 6A-B, C, D, E, F, 7A-B, C-D, 8A-B, C-D, 9E-F -- 39 entries, it would seem.

62. 10:1-6 (+ 11:2, 11:1,3): The striking trait of this thematically unitary set on rules of uncleanness applicable to the purification-rite is extended, complex, but smooth declarative sentences, 10:1A-C, D-E + F or G or H, 10:2A, B, C-E, F + G or H, 10:4A-C, D + E or F, 10:5G + H or I, J-L, 10:6A-C, (X which + verb + apocopated apodosis), H-I, J-K + L, M-Q -- evidently 15 entries in all. 11:2 certainly carries forward both the form and theme. 11:1 and 11:3 continue the theme, but not the form. 11:1-3 comprise an appendix.

63. 11:7-9: The unit on the hyssop is worked out in declarative sentences, generally brief and smooth ones. Disputing opinions take the form of glosses. I count these units: 11:7A, B, C, D, E-F, G, H + I, J-K, 8A, B, C, D-E + F; 9A-B + C, D-H, I-K -- 15 in all.

64. 12:1-6E, 8E-M, 9-11 (+ 12:6F, 7-8D -- see ii 14): This subdivision on sprinkling is unitary in theme and form, once we recognize and remove the unit formed by 12:6F-9. The specified set is in declarative sentences. Those at 12:1-3 are fully worked out and complex, with 12:2 and 3 requiring an understood if to conform. 12:4A shifts to the he-who, with the remainder reverting to the smooth and generally unapocopated construction characteristic at the outset, 12:4B-F, 12:5, and 12:6A-E. 12:10A + B or C form similarly smooth sentences, "The cover which ... is connected ..." 12:10D, E-F, and G are simple sentences. 12:11A, B-D require if, and E-F and G are simple. 12:8F-I, J, K, L. follow suit, so too 12:9. I discern the following units: 12:1A, B, 2A-C, D-E, F-H, I-K, L-N, O-P, Q-R, S, T, 3A-B, C-D, E-F, G-H, I, J, 4A, B, C-D, E-F, 5A, B, C-E, 6A-C, D-E, 8E, F-H, I, J, K, L + M, 9, 10A + B or C, D, E-G, 11A, B-D, E, F, G -- 40 in all.

Tohorot

65. 1:1-3 (+ 4): This item is an extended list. Thirteen rules on the carrion of the clean bird, 1:1-2, the carrion of the unclean bird, then 1:4, and with regard to cattle. The lists are not internally balanced. The whole serves as proem; though the theme is not then taken up, the principle is. M. 8:6 reverts to the issue and form.

66. 3:1-4: The issue is susceptibility of a substance as food and as liquid. The formulary preference is not fully articulated, but simple, declarative sentences. 3:1D + E-J are matched at 3:2D-H and 3:3A-E, F-J, four closely balanced sets. The whole construction inaugurated at 1:1 ends at 3:4, again simple, but extended, declarative sentences.

67. 3:5-8: The first set on matters of doubt, not explicitly referring to "it is a doubt whether ... it is a doubt whether ... not ...," is expressed in simple declarative sentences, 3:5A + B, C, D, 3:6A, B, C-D, 3:7A, B, C, 3:8A-C + D (dispute, 3 stichs), E-H, I-J + K, L-M -- 15 entries.

68. 4:1-6: The second set on matters of doubt shifts to lightly apocopated declarative sentences. 4:1A-D (he who ... it is ...), E-F (a loaf among keys, it is unclean, etc.); 4:2A-D, 4:3A(or B) + C(or D) + E-F, G-K, 4:4A-D, E-F, G-H, 4:5A (list), C, D, E, (dispute), 4:6A-F, G, H-K -- evidently 15 entries.

69. 4:7-13: this unit is explicitly formulated as an intermediate division, 4:7A: These are matters of doubt which sages have declared clean + 12 entries; then each entry is cited and explained. The predominant formulary pattern is cases stated in apocopation, the remaining items being in brief declarative sentences.

70. 5:1-6: The first intermediate division on doubts in the public domain is worked out in highly apocopated sentences, e.g., two paths ... he walked in one of them and it is not known ... clean/unclean, etc. 5:1-2 conclude with disputes and are matched. 5:3-4 are closely matched, likewise 5:5-6. The whole subdivision therefore is composed of three carefully matched pairs of pericopae, a masterful work of redaction. The pairs of course may belong as three separate entries at ii 18-20, but I am inclined to see them as a deliberately formed, whole intermediate division.

71. 5:7-9, 6:1: The next intermediate division on doubts in the public domain is worked out in complete declarative sentences, often requiring an unstated if. The entries are 5:7A-D, E-G (dispute), H-K, 5:8A-D, E-I; 5:9A-B, C-E, F-H, I-K, L-O -- clearly 10 in all. Then 6:1, in sizable declarative sentences, yields 6:1A-B, C, D-F, G, and H -- 5 more.

72. 6:2-4: The third subdivision on doubts in the public domain exhibits marked apocopation, 6:2A: Four matters of doubt does Joshua declare unclean and do sages declare clean + 4 simple sentences, cut off from one another + G, it is a matter of doubt re touching, H, overshadowing, I, moving + J-K, dispute-apodosis. 6:3 then gives the following apocopated sentences: A-D, E-G, H-J, K-L, M-P, 5 in all. 6:4 is built out of 6 stichs, 6:4A-C, generalization, D, how so, then E-F, G-H, I-J, K-L, M-N, O-Q + gloss, R-S.

73. 6:5-9: The fourth and last subdivision on doubts in public domain, now with regard to domain which sometimes is public, sometimes private, is in simple declarative sentences, 6:5A-C, protasis, completed by D or E, apodosis of a dispute; 6:6A + B + C + D, E-G, glossed by H, I, 6:7, 6:8A-B, C-E, 6:9A-D, E, F -- (probably) 20 entries in all.

74. 7:1-9, 8:1-5: The haber/^{C}am ha'ares unit is expressed in declarative sentences beginning he-who ... + verb + apocopated apodosis, 7:1A-C + D, E-F, 7:2A-D (+ E-G), 7:3, 7:4A-C (+ D-I), 7:5, 7:6A-E, F-G (+ H-L), 7:7A-C, D (+ E), 7:8, 7:9, 8:1, 8:2, 8:3A-G, H-N, 8:4, 8:5 -- 18 units beginning he-who ... In fact, with or without disputes, secondary glosses, explanations, and the like, the entire unit on the stated subject is laid out in exactly the same predominant formulary trait at the outset of each of its units.

75. 9:1-7: The announced topic, olives, is worked out in a series of dispute-pericopae, 9:1, 9:(2-3B +) 3C-K, 9:4, 9:5, 9:6-7, 9:6 setting the stage for 9:7, just as 9:2-3B does for 9:3C-K. There are, in all, 5 basic dispute-entries. If we now differentiate among the sentences yielded by the disputes of the intermediate division, we find the following: 9:1A-D -- duplicated subject (+ G, H); 9:2A-F, a long sentence, with if understood; G-H (+ I), the same; 9:3A, simple sentence; B-C (if understood) then ... is clean/unclean + Simeon's gloss, which is a long but smooth sentence; 9:4A-B, he who ... should give, D + E; 9:5A-C, He who ... lo, these are ... (+ D-F); G-H: He who ... has rendered ...; 9:6A-C, He who ... they are not ..., + declarative sentence, D-G, H-I (if understood, 2x); 9:7A + B-C, [if] ... let him ..., D, E, simple sentences. Accordingly, it is difficult to discern an clearcut pattern in the unit as a whole. It appears to me that we have 15 distinct entries in the intermediate division.

76. 9:8-9: The dead creeping thing in the press is the theme of this subdivision, stated in declarative sentences, 9:8A-B, C-D, E-F, G-I, 9:9A-B, C-E, F-G, H, I-J, K-M + N -- 10 in all, brief but smooth entries.

77. 10:1-3: The status of the workers in the olivepress (grape-gatherers, added at 10:2E and 10:3A) completes the thematic triology on olives. We should expect that a unit on the haber/^{C}am ha'ares will make use of the he-who-declarative sentence, and so we find at 10:1A (+ dispute), F, 10:5A, 10:6A, 10:7A -- 5. 10:5D-N are to be compared to 3:1D-J, 3:2D-H, 3:3D-J. We see that what is primary to tradental work on the four pericopae, that is the stated stichs, is secondary to redactional work which links one pericope to the next. Out 5 he-who's are as expected. 10:8 is tacked on, a set of smooth declarative sentences, 10:8A, B, C, D-E, F-H, K-I, L -- 7.

78. 10:4-7 (+10:8): The he-who-formulary characterizes the intermediate division on grapes and wine, 10:4A (+ dispute), F, 10:5A, 10:6A, 10:7A-5. 10:5D-N are to be compared to 3:1D-J, 3:2D-H, 3:3D-J. We see that what is primary to tradental work on the four pericopae, that is the stated stichs, is secondary to redactional work which links one pericope to the next. Our 5 he-who's are as expected. 10:8 is tacked on, as a set of smooth declarative sentences, 10:8A, B, C, D-E, F-H, I-K, L -- 7.

Miqvaot

79. 2:1-3: The intermediate division on doubts in connection with the immersion-pool is expressed in the apocopation characteristic of the equivalent subdivisions at M. Tohorot. We have the following units: 2:1, 2:2A-E, I-O, 2:3 -- 3 fundamental, but heavily glossed and complex, sets of apocopated clauses forming complete thoughts. The predominant redactional formulary trait of the following intermediate division, he-who or that-which + verb + (lightly) apocopated apodosis, is at 2:1A, 2:2A, and 2:3A, again 3 exempla.

80. 2:5-10 (+ 2:4): The intermediate division is marked by the he-who or that-which pattern of apocopation, 2:5A, 2:6A, 2:7A, 2:8A, 2:9A, 2:10A -- 6 in all. 2:4 is a simple dispute, introducing the theme at 2:5ff., which is the empty pool or the empty jar and the status of water collected therein.

81. 3:1-4: The sudivision is devoted to the point at which unfit water becomes fit, or fit water unfit. There are two striking formulary traits, he who or that which, 3:1A, G, 3:2B, 3:3A, 3:3E, 3:3H, I, 3:4C, D -- 9 in all; and apocopation in consequence of some, though not all, of these inaugural entries. I separate 3:1-4 from the following set because the theme shifts.

82. 4:1-5, 5:1-3: The principal theme is collecting water for the immersion pool. The dominant formulary pattern is he who or that which + mild apocopation, 4:1A-D, 4:2A, 4:3A-C, 4:4A-E, 4:5A (+ B-F) (note that the second entry, G [+ H-L] does not repeat the that which formulary), 5:1A (+ B-H, 5:2), and 5:3A -- 7 in all.

83. 5:4-5, 5:6: The common theme is water which bears the traits of spring-water as against that which bears the traits of immersion-pool water. 5:4 contains three well-articulated declarative sentences, set forth as a dispute. 5:5A and B comprise two more -- 5 in all. There are an intruded sentence, 5:5C, and two more, 5:5D-G and H, which continue 5:5A, B. 5:6 then gives five declarative sentences, A-B, D-E, F, G + H + I (a dispute), and J.

84. 6:1-11: The common theme is intermingling of waters, and the single characteristic formulary trait is declarative sentences, not marked by extreme apocopation. A case can be made for the inclusion of 5:6G-J in this unit, since it forms a transition from the foregoing. The complete sentences are as follows: 6:1A, B-C, C (+ E-G); 6:2A-B, C-E; 6:3A-I (apocopated), J-N; 6:4, 6:5A-C, D, E-G, H, I-J; 6:6A-D, E-F, G-J (apocopation), K-L; 6:7A-C, D-H, I + J; 6:8A-C, D + E-H, I-L; 6:9A-C + D, E; 6:10A-E, F, G (dispute); 6:11A-D (+ E-F), G-J -- 30 in all, it would appear.

85. 7:1-2: There are things which raise a pool and do not invalidate it, invalidate and do not raise, do not raise and do not invalidate -- a fine triple-generalization followed by the expected lists, 7:1D-E + F-M; 7:2N-T, U-BB, common theme and redactional formulary. But the entries do not closely match in internal formulation.

86. 7:3-5: The unitary theme is colored liquids in an immersion pool. 7:4-5 present their ideas in mild apocopation, 7:4A-C; 7:5A-E, F-J (matching) + K -- 3 entries in all. 7:3 is in simple declarative sentences.

87. 7:6-7: Apocopation characterizes this set, devoted to the immersion in the pool, 7:6A-C, 7:7E-J, K-N, again three base-units. The rest is in simple declarative sentences.

88. 8:1 + 2-4 (+ 8:5): This unit is spun out, one theme and form generating the next. 8:1 itself is an intermediate division, 8:1A-C, D, E-F, three base-entries, all in simple declarative sentences, on the immersion-pools in the Land and otherwise, Israelite and gentile. The reference therein to those unclean with seminal issue causes the redactor to append a further intermediate division, also in declarative sentences, on those who have had an emission and require immersion. 8:5 continues the formulary pattern of simple and smooth declarative sentences; its subject is the immersion of the menstruating woman, and its principle is interposition, a transition from 8:1-4 to Chapter Nine. The unifying theme of the whole -- Chapters Eight through Ten -- is use of the pool, with emphasis, at 8:5ff., on interposition.

89. 9:1-7: Formally parallel to 7:1-2, this intermediate division consists of a simple formulary pattern, the list, on a single theme, interposition. But since the entries on the list are diverse, we cannot regard the formulary pattern of the components as internal to the construction. It is clearly redactional, not tradental, in that diverse formulary units on a single theme are united by the encompassing construction. The subunits are four: 9:1-2, These interpose on man; 9:3-4, These do not interpose; 9:5, These interpose on utensils; 9:6, On garments.

90. 10:1-8: The unitary theme is use of the immersion-pool, with special reference to interposition. The single formulary pattern is declarative sentences, nearly all of them rather long and smoothly articulated. There are several clearly demarcated subunits, 10:1 (10:1A-D, E-F, G-H, I, J, K, L), 10:2-4 (marked off by the apodosis, require that water enter into them), 10:2A, B, C; 10:3A-B, 10:4C-D (matched), E-F. 10:5A-C, D-E, F-G, H form further declarative units, some set forth as disputes. 10:6 is a further subunit, A-B (dispute), C-E + F. 10:7 presents three long sentences, A, B, C-D; 10:8 gives the following: 10:8A-C, D-E, F-G, H-I, J -- evidently 27 in all. Even though we clearly

discern diverse kinds of declarative sentences and subunits, I think the whole constitutes a single intermediate division, united by theme and externally-unitary formal traits.

Niddah

91. 1:1-7: The theme of this intermediate division is the resolution of doubts concerning objects a woman has touched before the onset of her period. The dominant formulary trait is the dispute, 1:1A-C + D, 1:3, 1:4I-M, 1:5P-Q. But there is a further unifying characteristic, which is the repeated citation and gloss of principal pericopae, 1:1 at 1:2, 7; 1:3 at 1:4-5, 6. The declarative sentences exhibit these traits: 1:1A, matched by B: duplicated subject ("All women ... sufficient for them is ..."); D-F, G (duplicated subject), H + I, She who ..., lo, this is ... (mild apocopation); 1:2A + B-C, D; E (simple sentences); 1:3A-B, Four woman ... + list, C, D (simple sentences); 1:4E, Who is ... + F, G + H, I + J (matched triplet); K-L (If understood + simple sentence + M); 1:4N-O (Who is ...); P, Q (duplicated subject in both); 1:6A-B (And of what case ... in the case of); C,D (simple sentences), 7:7A-C Even though ..., she must ... except ..., D-F (in the model of the foregoing), G-I, J + K -- 25 entries in all.

92. 2:1-7: These general rules on menstrual uncleanness are phrased as simple declarative sentences, 2:1A, B-C, D-E; 2:2A-C + 2:3D-F, G + H; 2:4A, B, C-E; 2:5A-B, C, D; 2:6A-B, C + D, E-G, H-I; 2:7J-K, L-M + N, O-P, Q-R, S-U -- evidently 20 in all.

93. 3:1-7: This intermediate division, on the status of abortions, exhibits a striking redactional form, she who produces, 3:1A, 3:2A, 3:3A, 3:4A, 3:5A (understood at 3:5C, E), 3:6A, 3:7A -- 9 in all, counting the understood but unstated exempla. The apodosis in each case is a declarative sentence.

94. 4:1-3: We find another set of declarative sentences, 4:1A, B-F; 4:2A-B, C (dispute); 4:3A-B + C or D, E + F or G + H -- 5 principal thoughts expressed in distinct sentence-units. The theme is uncleanness of non-Israelite women in respect to menstruation.

95. 4:4-6 + 7 (5:1-2): The declarative sentence continues, she who is in labor, 4:4A, 4:6A. 4:5 carries forward and glosses 4:4. 4:7(+ 5:1-2, below, No. 96) completes the intermediate division, 3 basic entries. In simple declarative sentences, general rules on the eleven days of Zibah, introduced at 4:4-6, are laid out, 4:7A, B-F + G, H-I, J-L.

96. 5:1-2: This set is united by simple declarative sentences, 5:1A-C, D, E-F, G; 5:2H-I, J-L -- six base-units, and by the fact that Simeon is the authority of the intermediate division. There is no common theme, rather a single authority.

97. 5:7-9, 6:1, 6:11-12: The unit deals with signs of maturity. The whole is in declarative sentences, 5:7A-C, D, E; 5:8F-J (diverse answers to a single question), 5:9A-B, C, D-E, F (+ G), H, I-J; 6:1A, B + C or D, E (which is redactional and links 6:1 to 6:2-10) -- 12 entries + 6:1E. 6:11-12 resume the matter interrupted by the apophthegmatic construction of 6:2-10 (iv 2). The simple but balanced declarative sentences continue at 6:11A-B, C-F, G + H -- three entries. 6:12 glosses the matter of the two hairs, tacked on for thematic reasons.

98. 6:13-14, 7:1-5, 8:1-4, 9:1-10: This sizable intermediate division is united by a common theme, doubts in connection with menstrual blood. Its formulary coherence is gross, not refined, consisting as it does of declarative sentences of several types. Nonetheless, given the single theme and the single gross thematic preference, I think we are on fairly solid ground in treating the set as a single subdivision, itself composed of sizable units of material as follows: 6:13A she who sees ..., (a whole sentence), B, C (a dispute phrased in complete, unbalanced sentences, B completing A, C standing by itself); 6:14A-C, D, she who sees + a further observation; 7:1A-B, C-D, E-F, G-I, (sizable and well-articulated declarative sentences); 7:2A-C, D-F, G (as above); 7:3A + B, C, D-F (disputes in whole sentences); 7:4A, B (well-articulated sentences); 7:5A, B, C, D, E (as above); 8:1A-C, she who sees ... if ... unclean, and if ... clean, D, E-G, H, I-J, K-N; 8:2A, And she blames it ..., B-D, E-F, G-H, I1, I2, J, K-Q (ma^{C}aseh -- one entry); 8:4A-C, 9:1A + B (C responds to B), the woman who; 9:2A-D, a man or woman who ..., (+ dispute as above); 9:3A-B, a woman lent ..., lo, this one ..., D-F, G-H + I; 9:4A-B, Three women who ... all are unclean; C-D, E; 9:5A-B (as above); H, I, J, K-O, P + Q; 9:6-7: Seven substances + list, 9:6A B, C-E, F, G, H, I J, K; 9:8A -- any woman who has a fixed period ... sufficient (=1:1,7), B-D, And these are the tokens, E; 9:9A-B [If] she usually ... (fully articulated sentences), 9:9C-D vs. E, (dispute in complete sentences; 9:10F-G, H, I-J, K, L -- 70 (!) entries in all, it would seem. Self-evidently, this large intermediate division yields the following subdivisions: 6:13-14, 7:1; 7:2; 7:3-4 + 5; 8:1-2 + 3, 4; 9:1-2; 9:3; 9:4-5; 9:6-7; 9:8-10 -- 10 in all. The common theme announced at 6:13 and concluded through 9:10 and the persistence of a simple formulary preference -- to be sure, in diverse versions -- in my judgment justifies treating the whole as one vast intermediate division, parallel in its way to that on the haber/^{C}am ha'ares, above No. 74.

99. 9:11, 10:1-8: 9:11 is a prologue to the subsequent construction, a simple but extended declarative sentence. The dominant redactional-formulary trait is he-who or she-who, 10:1A a girl whose time ..., they give her; 10:2A, a menstruating woman who ..., lo, she is ...; 10:3A. The Zab and Zabah who ..., lo, they are; 10:5A, a woman who died ..., it [blood] ...; 10:6A, [at first ...], She who ... did pour ...; 10:8A, she who sees and immersed ..., they impart ... -- 6 entries. The unit further is marked by well-balanced disputes, 10:1A-C, D-G, H-J (Houses); 10:2H-J (Judah); 10:3 (Eliezer, Joshua, ^{C}Aqiva); 10:4D-F (Houses); 10:5 (Judah, Yose); 10:6, 7 (Houses, 2x); 10:8A-C, D-F, + G (Houses). The general theme is the uncleanness of menstrual blood under diverse special circumstances.

Makhshirin

100. 1:1 + 1:2-6: After the opening generalization, declarative sentences, 1:1A-C + D, the unit works out its ideas in he-who or that-which sentences, normally with an apocopated dispute-apodosis, It is (+/- not) under, etc. The theme of the chapter is water which is wanted at some point, or under some circumstance, but not at some other, just as 1:1 announces. The units are 1:2, 1:3, 1:4 (Houses-disputes, 3x); 1:5, 1:6A-C, D-G, H-I -- 7 in all, 2 groups of 3, and 1:5, thus 3 principal entries in all.

101. 2:1-2 + 2:3A-D: Rules on sweat of houses, etc., are given in simple declarative sentences, 2:1A-B, C, D, E; 2:2A-B, C-E -- 6 in all. 2:3A-D links 2:1-2 to the formulary construction 2:2E-11. The other entries diverge in obvious ways.

102. 3:1-4:5: The common theme is the status of objects, particularly food, which absorb liquid under various circumstances. The recurrent formulary pattern to inaugurate units is he-who or that which + the usual apodosis, it is under (+/- not), or, occasionally, unclean/clean. The units are 3:1A-E (+ F-G), 3:2A-D (E-H), 3:3A + B or C or D-E (dispute, declares unclean, etc.), 3:4A-D, E-G, H; 3:5A-C, D, E-F, G-I (+ 3:6J-N); 3:7O-Q, 3:8A-B, C-E; 4:1A-C, D-E; 4:2, 4:3, 4:4A-E, 4:5F-J, P-R -- 20 entries in all.

103. 4:6-10, 5:1-6: The theme shifts to the insusceptibility of food, or other objects, even though it is wet. The pattern shifts too. The he-who or that-which protasis yields in the main apocopation: 4:6A-B, 4:7A-C, 4:8A-C (no apocopation at all), 4:6A-B + C, 4:10A-B (no apocopation at all0, 5:1A-B, 5:2A-C, 5:3 (apocopation), 5:4A-C (continued at 5:5), 5:6A-C -- 15 items in all.

104. 5:7-8 + 9: The basic formulary is a catalogue of items + is +/- not under the law, etc. 5:7A (3+), B (3+), D-G (he who, 3x) -- three sets. 6:8 has 2 items + is not, etc., and 5:9 is an appended declarative sentence, out of phase both formally and thematically. Since 5:10 starts a new subdivision, it seems probable that 5:9 has been dropped into place with little regard for formal cogency.

105. 5:10-11, 6:1-2C: We revert to he-who and its equivalents, with an apocopated predicate clean = not under, etc. The units are 5:10A-F, 5:11A-H, J-L, 6:1A-C, 6:2A-C -- 5 in all.

106. 6:2D-H, 3: The striking formulary pattern, smooth declarative sentences beginning all and exhibiting no apocopation whatsoever, is applied to the status as to susceptibility, because of chance wetting down, of various kinds of food. The units are 6:2D, G; 6:3A, D, F -- 5 in all.

107. 6:4-7 + 8: The concluding unit consists of two catalogues, 6:4-5, and 6:6-7, both fairly tightly articulated. They deal with fluids which do or do not impart susceptibility to uncleanness. The first, 6:4A-B, lists 7 fluids which do, then adding subspecies of blood and water, and further glossing the basic list. 6:6A, These impart uncleanness and susceptibility to uncleanness at once (reverting to 1:1C), and 6:7A. These do not become unclean and do not impart susceptibility to uncleanness, are closely matched as well -- 1 + 2 = three principal components in all. 6:8 is tacked on, being thematically relevant but formally discrete.

Zabim

108. 1:1-6: The inaugural unit is built upon the recurrent use of see, in two sections, he who sees + disputes, 1:1A-C, 1:2A-C; and [if] he saw, 1:3A, 1:4A, D, 1:5A, E, 1:6A, G -- 3 + 7, 10 in all. The unifying theme is the definition of the ages at which a man becomes a Zab.

109. 2:1-4: General rules on the Zab -- who becomes one, how he is examined, his susceptibility to flux, and how he imparts uncleanness, are stated as simple declarative

sentences. 2:1, All are susceptible + lists; 2:2, In seven ways do they examine the Zab + list; 2:3, He who sees semen does not ..., a gentile who saw ..., she who sees (+ 2 further sayings built on twenty-four hours); 2:4, The Zab imparts uncleanness to the bed in 5 ways, bed to man in 7 -- thus 3 lists.

110. 3:1-3: This intermediate division consists of two closely matched sets. First are 3:1A, D-N = 3:3A, D-K+L, which deal with the effects of the Zab's and clean person's sitting on infirm as against firm bases. The second is 3:2, itself a composite of balanced sub-sets, 3:2A-B, C-D, E-G, G-I, J-L -- 5 if-sentences, concluded at M. The theme is the same, namely, the consequences of the Zab's and the clean person's exerting pressure together. 3:3L-P resumes the if construction of 3:2. The redaction obviously involves two prior units, as I said, but we clearly have a complete and intentionally demarcated intermediate division.

111. 4:1-7: This complex unit makes use of two types of sentence, he-who, and [if] (something articulated). The theme is the same as the foregoing, the pressure of the Zab. The he-who exempla are 4:1A, E, and 4:4A. That yields 3 basic units. The if-sentences, which inaugurate fresh units of thought, not dependent on a he-who protasis, are at 4:2A, 4:3A, 4:5D (continued at 4:6A), 4:7A (continued at 4:7C-F), and 4:7G -- 5 basic units. As at No. 110, it would appear that the redactor has chosen to intertwine two originally distinct (proto) intermediate divisions (!). The principal point of confusion is at 4:4A. If we take account of the fact that 4:4A-C are integral to Simeon's group, 4:4-5, we have a different division entirely: 4:1 -- Joshua; 4:2 [if a Zab knocked] against + 9 entries = 1, 4:3A-D [If he knocked] against + 5 + 2 + 1 + 3, 4:3F, against + 3 -- 24 predicates of against; 4:4-5 + 6A, Simeon, and 4:7; [If] sentences at A-B, C, D-F, G, H, as specified above. Accordingly, it would appear that the set, which clearly is to be demarcated from Chapters Three and Five, is a composite of materials assigned to particular authorities, 4:1, 4:4-6A, and materials organized around formulary preferences, 4:2-3, 7. To be sure, the whole lot is in declarative sentences, but a case could be made for setting the subdivision at v 14.

112. 5:1-5: The unitary theme is ways in which the Zab imparts uncleanness, not solely through pressure, as at 110-111, but also through touching and shifting. The unitary formulary trait is long, fully articulated declarative sentences, which are to be distinguished from one another in groups, as follows: 5:1A-D, E-M (Joshua), 5:2B-E, 5:2G-P (a very tight unit, [If] ..., he ... [when] ..., G-I, J-K, L-M, N-O, P -- 5 in all), 5:3B-C, D-E, G-I (Whatever ..., except ... --3 in all), 5:4-5, Simeon's group, [If] ... he is unclean (5:4A, B, D, D + E vs. 5:4F, G -- 6 entries), 5:5 continuing the foregoing, If ... unclean, (A, B). A good case could be made for the inclusion of 5:2, 5:3, and 5:4-5B, as three separate divisions, in which internally-unitary formulary traits characterize distinctive thematic units.

Tebul Yom

113. 1:1-2: The theme persists through several intermediate divisions, distinguished from one another by a shift in formulary pattern. That theme is connection in regard to

the Tebul Yom. The first is characterized by the he-who-construction of its inaugural clauses, 1:1A, F (preceded by D-E), 1:2A + B -- 3 in all.

114. 1:3-5: The second intermediate division, on the stated theme, is marked by simple declarative sentences, commencing with a sizable subject, e.g., a list of several items + are made unclean by the Tebul Yom, 1:3, 1:4, 1:5A-B, F-G (a matched pair) -- 3 in all.

115. 2:1-4:4: The third division, built in he-who or that-which clauses, on the stated theme, reverses the subject and predicate, a cooking pot which ... if it was ... the liquids are ..., followed by the normal sequence of subject and predicate, and if ... all is ... The formulary preference is to place at the outset of the sentence the principal topic, whether or not it syntactically belongs at the head of the declarative sentence, as follows (grouping complete thoughts): 2:1A-F; 2:2A-G; 2:3A-E; 2:4; 2:5A-C, F-G, H-I or J; 2:6A-C, 2:7A-B; 2:8A-D; 3:1B + C (as above); 3:2A-C; 3:3A-B; 3:4E-F + G (dispute); 3:5A-B + C (as above); 3:6A-C (clearcut apocopation), 4:1A-D; 4:2; 4:3; 4:4A-C -- 20 units in all.

Yadayim

116. 1:1-2:4: The unit on the rules of washing hands is composed of simple declarative sentences, 1:1A-D, G; 1:2A-B, C, D, E, F; 1:3A-C, D E-G; 1:4A-C, D-F, 1:5A-B, C, D, E-F; 2:1A + B-C, D + E; 2:2A-D + E-F; 2:3A, C, D, E, F, G, H, I-J; 2:4A-D, E, (+ 2:4H-U [H-I, J-K, L-N, O-Q, R-T, 5 in all + U] -- 30 + 5 = 35 (!) in all.

117. 3:1-2: The set devoted to the remove of uncleanness attributed to hands is constructed in disputes, as follows: 3:1A-C, D-F (+ G-H); I-J (+ K-L); 3:2A-C -- 4 in all, 2 for ^CAqiva, 2 for Joshua.

118. 3:3-5, 4:5: This intermediate division, on Scriptures which impart uncleanness to hands, is expressed in simple declarative sentences, 3:3A (+ B, C-D -- disputes); 3:4A (+ B), 3:5A-C, D-F, G, H (+ I-S); 4:5A, B, C -- 9 in all.

Uqsin

119. 1:1-4, 6 (+ 5): This major intermediate division presents a set of three generalizations, Whatever is a handle but not ... contracts but does not join together; if it ... it contracts and imparts and joins ... If it is not ... and not ... it does not ... and does not .... Then the generalizations are systematically illustrated through lists and finally are repeated, 1:2 = 1:1B, 1:3 = 1:1A, 1:4 = 1:1C. 1:6A-C = 1:1B, 1:6E-I = 1:1A, 1:6J = 1:1C. Interpolated is 1:5, a triplet, C-D, E-F, and H-I. We appear to have 3 triplets -- 9.

120. 2:1-4: The unit on uncleanness of foods is stated in declarative sentences, 2:1A-B, C + D; 2:2A + 2:4A (+ 2), 2:2B-C, D, E-F, G-H + I-L, 2:3A-B, C-E, 2:4B-E -- 12 in all.

121. 2:5-6 + 7-8: The primary unit on disconnection, 2:5-6, consists of 5 units, declarative sentences inaugurated by he-who, but then worked out in simple and smooth syntax (see Part XX, p. 25): 2:5A-C, D-F, 2:6A-B, C, D (+ 2:6E-H) -- 5 in all.

122. 2:9-10: The intermediate division on the plant in the pot is in declarative sentences, 2:9A, B-C, 2:10A, B-C, D-E, F -- six units in all.

123. 3:1-3 + 9: The set on preparation and intention in relation to the susceptibility of foods, like No. 119, opens with a major generalization, which then is systematically illustrated, 3:1A = 3:1E, 3:1B = 3:2, 3:1C = 3:3A-C, 3:1D + 3:3D-G -- 5 exempla. The illustrations do not follow a single formulary pattern. 3:9 resumes the theme and contrasts things which require preparation and those which do not.

124. 3:4-7: The intermediate division on produce which serves as food but is not subject to tithes, etc., is worked out in simple declarative sentences, some of them composed of the protasis and a stich of the disputed apodosis, 3:4A, B, 3:5A + B-C, D, 3:6A + B, C, D, E or F, G + H or I, 3:7A-C, D -- 10 in all.

125. 3:8, 10-11: The intermediate division on whether we deem what is bound to happen as if it already has happened is constructed of disputes, 3:8A-D, E-G; 3:10 (which introduces 3:11, yields 1); 3:11 -- treating 3:10 + 11 as one entry, 3 in all (or otherwise, 4).

    iv.   Intermediate Divisions Defined by Cogent Themes but Lacking Formulary Coherence

Thirteen intermediate divisions clearly focus upon a single problem or theme but lack externally-unitary formulary traits. These items are particularly interesting because, as we shall observe, the distinct cognitive units do exhibit familiar formulary traits, e.g., matched lists, disputes, disciplined declarative sentences, and the like. But as a group, they do not seem to me to contain traces of an effort to link the several cognitive units into a common pattern or to impose upon them a single formulary trait of redactional consequence, however minor. The operative distinction between tradental and redactional forms and formulary patterns is best illustrated in the present catalogue.

Kelim

1. 14:1-8: While the individual segments of this unit follow well-established and familiar forms, the unit as a whole does not exhibit formulary congruence. 14:1 is a set of answers to a question; 14:2 is a set of declarative sentences, so too 14:3. I see no clearcut pattern. 14:4-5 are lists, unclean parts of the wagon, clean parts, 10 vs. 8. 14:6-7 + 8A-B are disputes, the remainder are simple declarative sentences. The common theme is metal utensils. Chapter Fifteen is clearly delineated from this intermediate division, since it turns to wooden ones.

2. 18:1-3: This group treats the theme of the chest, with a dispute, 18:1, and a large, balanced unit of highly disciplined declarative sentences, 18:2, then another dispute, 18:3A-E. The disputes yield simple sentences, 18:1, The box ... is measured ...; 18:3, the box, etc., one of whose legs ... are ... clean ... But I see no match or balance among the three primary entries.

3. 19:1-4: The uniting theme is the bed-rope and bed-girth. The set clearly carries forward the foregoing, in general, but not in detail. Components exhibit no common pattern, though they adhere to familiar forms used in the formal construction of

autonomous units. 19:2 and 19:3 are linked by x which goes forth (HYWS') from the bed; 19:4 then has an implied if.

4. 23:2-5: The components of the unit exhibit a fine and well-crafted formulary structure, 23:2: These are + 5; 23:3: That is the difference; 23:4: two sets of 3 items; 23:5: 5 items vs. 3. But there is no predominant formal preference. It is not a set of formal lists. The cogent theme is midras-uncleanness and its modes.

5. 26:1-9: The group is united by the theme, leather objects. The individual entries again conform to established tradental formulary patterns: 26:1, list with glosses; 26:2, x/unclean, y/clean; 26:3, clean/unclean, unclean/clean; 26:4 = 18:5-9; 26:5, list; 26:6, dispute; 26:7, balanced declarative sentences; 26:8, balanced declarative sentences; 26:9, dispute. But there is not a trace of an effort to impose redactional-formal ties upon the units.

6. 27:5, 6: The common theme is the size at which cloth is susceptible to uncleanness. 27:5A-D, F-I present disputes, 26:6, a list: These are measured double.

7. 28:3, 4: The theme is fabrics. 28:3 is in diverse sentences, 28:4, a dispute. These are not closely linked.

8. 28:9, 10: The theme is diverse objects made of fabric. There is no common form.

9. 30:1-4: The common theme is glass utensils. 30:1A-C: See vii 1. 30:1D-E: Balanced declarative sentence. B-C contain a ma^{C}aseh, then colloquy. 16:2A-F is in apocopation, as an example should be -- 3 units(?).

Negaim

11. 7:2-5, 8:1-10: The common and clearcut theme of 7:2-5 is how we deal with changes in a bright spot, whether these changes are natural or self-induced. 7:2 is in declarative sentences, which set up a dispute; 7:3 presents apocopated units, A-C, D-F, G-I, and J-L. 7:4 is a complex composition, primarily in declarative sentences, and 7:5 is a dispute, in less fully articulated sentences.

8:1-10 are certainly a thematic unit, and continue the problems inaugurated at 7:3, changes in the bright spot. The set also carries forward the mixture of declarative sentences and apocopated examples, but the layout is not so systematic, e.g., as at M. Oh. 6:1ff., to warrant classifying the whole as a single unit organized not only by theme but also around a single formulary pattern. 8:1 is a set of simple declarative sentences, lacking articulation. 8:2-3 present apocopated units, 8:2A-G + H-I, J-L; 8:3A-E, F-I + J-K -- 6. 8:4 reverts to the pattern of 8:1. 8:5A-B are fully articulated declarative sentences, followed by apocopated examples joined by how so? 8:6A-E form still another apocopated unit, but F-K and L-P are declarative sentences. 8:7 presents the same mixture, 8:7A, B, are declarative; 8:7C, D, E, apocopation; 8:8, 8:9, and 8:10A, declarative; 8:10B-E + F, G-K, exceedingly well matched apocopated clauses. Accordingly, the unit coheres through a single theme, but, while its formulary repertoire is disciplined as to its internal construction, it does not exhibit an effort at systematic formulary schematization of the whole. Nonetheless, an argument certainly could be constructed for inclusion of the set a iii 46. I see the following principal units: 7:2A-C, D-G; 7:3A-C, D-F, G-I, J-L; 7:4A, B-C, E-H, I-K; 7:5A, B-D, E; 8:1A-C, D-F, 2A-G, H-I, J-L, 3A-E, F-I, J, K, 4A-C, D-H, 5A, B, C-G, H-M, 6A-E, F-K, L, M, N-P, 7A, B, C-E, F, G, H-I, 8A-C, D, E, F, 9, 10A, B-E, F, G-J, K -- 50 in all, it would appear.

12. 10:1-9: We certainly must regard this set as a single intermediate division, centered as it is on the theme of scalls. As at No. 11, the unit is a mixture of declarative sentences (including disputes), 10:1, 2, 3A-F, 4, 5A-C, 8, 9, and apocopation, 10:3G-H, 5D-O, 6, 7 -- 11 units. The same factors which require setting No. 11 here apply to No. 12.

Parah

13. 5:5-9: The common theme, utensils used for mixing ash and water, is expressed in sets of fully articulated, matched sentences, 5:5, 5:7A-D, E-K; disputes, 5:6; apocopation, 5:8, 9. One could make a case that 5:1-4 belong here and not as a separate entry at iii 57.

Tohorot: None.

Miqvaot: None.

Niddah: None.

Makhshirin: None.

Zabim
14. See iii 111.

Tebul Yom: None.

Yadayim: None.

Uqsin: None.

v. Intermediate Divisions Defined by Unitary Formulary Traits but Lacking Coherent Themes

We have once more a very brief list, intermediate divisions clearly demarcated by unitary formulary traits but covering diverse themes. But the brief list may be too long. Nos. 1, 2, and 3 follow an internally-unitary formulary pattern, while Nos. 4 and 5 do not. The latter are autonomous cognitive units, joined by the briefest and most blatant redactional formulas. Moreover, No. 1 may be seen as a set for the list of inter-nally-unitary and thematically coherent subdivisions, since it does, after all, deal -- if in a gross way -- wholly with matters of uncleanness. Accordingly, there are only two subdivisions which wholly ignore substantive considerations and take shape around a highly disciplined, internally-unitary formulary pattern -- a negligible number.

Kelim: None.

Ohalot: None.

Negaim: None.

Parah

1. 8:2-7: The common formulary trait is apophthegmatic, What made you unclean did not make me unclean but you did ..., 8:2, 8:4, 8:5, 8:6, 8:7 -- five in all. The entries do not treat a common theme, apart from uncleanness in general, and invoke quite discrete rules.

Tohorot: None.

Miqvoat: None.

Niddah

2. 6:2-10: Again we have an apophthegmatic construction, in which a single recurrent clause links materials exhibiting a common internal formulary pattern and no coherence in theme. 6:1E introduces the set but is external it is, It is possible for X, not Y, but it is not possible for Y, not X. The apophthegm is, Whoever is X, Y, but there is one who is Y, not X. The units are 6:2B-C, D; 6:3; 6:4F, G; 6:5; 6:6; 6:7; 6:8; 6:9L, M; 6:10 -- 12 entries in all.

Makhshirin

3. 2:3-11: This construction in 14 major entries follows a very tight form: X + Y -- if greater part X, unclean, if greater part Y, clean, half and half, unclean. But the theme is diverse, not only cleanness, but fitness and other matters entirely. Of the 14 entries, the following adhere closely to the given form: 2:3E-H, I-L, M-P; 2:4A-F; 2:5A-E; 2:6A-D; 2:7A-D; 2:8A-D; 2:10A-D, E-H (Meir) -- 10 in all.

Zabim: None.

Tebul Yom: None.

Yadayim

4. 4:1-4: The sole connection is the redactional formula, On that day, 4:1A, 4:2A, H, 4:3A, 4:4A -- 5 in all, it would seem. There is no thematic unity.

5. 4:6-8: The redactional formula unites these diverse and thematically discrete items is Say X, we complain, etc., 4:6A-B, 4:7A-B, D, F, 4:8A, D -- 6 in all.

Uqsin: None.

vi. Intermediate Divisions Wholly Lacking Formal or Thematic Coherence and Defined Solely by Redactional Context

Our twin criteria for discerning the intermediate divisions of our Order fail in the following four items. (No. 6 is a cross-reference, No. 3 is included for the sake of completeness. No. 1 is simply a redactional anomaly.) No. 2 treats the common theme of the cleanness of utensils, first, with attention to substance, second, with stress on formal characteristics of utensils. The second group contradicts the view of the first, since M. Kel. 17:15-16 allege that any utensil, of whatever substance, is able to contain uncleanness, while M. Kel. 17:13-14 maintain that some substances are wholly insusceptible, and this without regard to the shape of form imposed upon them. The reason for joining M. Toh. 8:6-9 -- No. 5 -- is to be located in the subtle work of the ultimate redactors. Lacking all semblance of a common theme and form, the set nonetheless reveals a rather substantial redactional purpose. No. 7 is the sole item which certainly belongs on the present list, an intermediate division both devoted to diverse topics and lacking all significant formal unity.

Kelim

1. 5:4 is formally and thematically out of place. See ii 6.

2. 17:13-17: Clearly, 17:12 marks the end of a highly coherent formal unit, delineated also by a single theme. 18:1-3 deal with their own coherent problem, followed by another cogent set. In between, 17:13-17 are an utterly miscellaneous set, lacking a single theme and exhibiting diverse forms. 17:13-14 fit together in theme and form -- declarative sentences, clean substances. 17:15-16 deal with receptacles, the former in apocopated, the latter in smooth sentences. 17:17 also treats receptacles, in unclean/clean sequences. It is difficult to see the group as joined in form or theme. Yet the sequence of dialectical issues is not to be ignored -- clean substances, then receptacles of any substance. I count the following units: 17:13A-B, C, 14A, B, C, D-F, G, 15A, B, C, D, E, 16A-E + F, 17A, B, C, D-F, G, H, I -- 20 in all.

[3. 26:1-9: See iv 5. Certainly 25:9 marks the end of one subdivision of the tractate, and 27:1-2 begin a fresh one. There is a common theme, leather objects, so the principal criterion of subdivision is not contextual. I count the following units: 26:1A-D, E-F, 2A, B, C, D, E, F-H, 3A, B, C, D, E-G, 4A, B, C, D, E, F, G-I, J-K, L M, 5A-C, D-F, 6A, B-D, E-G, 7, 8A-D, E-H, 9A-C, D -- 33 in all.]

(4. 28:3-4: See v 7.)

Ohalot: None.

Negaim: None.

Parah: None.

Tohorot

5. 8:6-9: 8:6 deals in declarative sentences with intention in the susceptibility of uncleanness: 8:7 is a dispute on outer sides of a utensil made unclean by liquids; 8:8 turns to a set of lightly apocopated sentences on liquids on an incline, and 8:9 on the same theme, is a dispute. The redactional purpose in this set is discussed at Part XI, pp. 13-14. It is clear that the subdivision lacks both a common theme and a common formulary pattern, even though -- paradoxically -- the thoughtful and purposive character of the redactor of the unit is self-evident.

Miqvaot: None.

Niddah: None.

Makhshirin

6. See iii 104, re 5:9.

Zabim: None.

Tebul Yom

7. 4:5-7: 4:5A-B, C-D are joined by, At first ... they reverted ... 4:6A, B are simple declarative sentences, linked by Joshua's reference, C. 4:7 has further declarative sentences, but their pattern ignores the foregoing. The themes of the several units are entirely out of phase with one another.

Yadayim: None.

Uqsin: None.

vii. Intermediate Divisions Originally Defined by Internally-Unitary Formulary Traits and Coherent Themes but Split Apart for Redactional Purposes

It remains to take note of negative redaction, that is, the work of taking apart a highly disciplined intermediate division and inserting into it diverse materials or using its elements for a purpose other than that for which they were originally formulated and put together. There are four principal exempla of this phenomenon, not a great many. I am not sure that No. 1 originally constituted a complete unit. It can have been made up to serve precisely its present purpose. Nos. 3 and 5 are the best examples of the phenomenon. No. 6 represents a rather gross one. In all, the deliberate disintegration of well-formed intermediate divisions is not commonplace.

Kelim

1. 2:1, 11:1, 15:1A-E, 36:1A-C: These pericopae follow a single, tight pattern and, if set together, would form a chapter organized around an internally-unitary formulary pattern and a coherent theme. As they stand, the units inaugurate separate large thematic subdivisions of intermediate units in Kelim. Each is formally independent of its present setting.

2. 2:2A-C, 2:3A, 2:7A-C: See iii 1.

3. 27:7, 8, 10 (+ 9), 11, 12, 28:1, 2, 7, 8 (+ 28:6?): This group, using the formulary 3 x 3 which, certainly exhibits a common theme as well, a piece of cloth 3 x 3 hand-breadths. 27:9 is intruded because it was joined to 27:10 before the doublet joined the 3 x 3 construction, to which 27:10A is integral. The formulary is at 27:7A, 8A, M, N, 10C, 11A, 12A, C, G, 28:1A, B, 2A, 7A, 8A, C -- 15 in all, a good unit. (28:6 seems to demand a 3 x 3 formulary at A, but forms a unit with 28:5.)

Ohalot

4. 2:1A-B, 3A-D, 5A-B: See iii 26.

Negaim: None.

Parah: None.

Tohorot: None.

Miqvaot

5. 1:1A + B, 1:6 A + B, 1:7A + B-C, D + E-I, 1:7, 1:8: The unit clearly was intended as a set of carefully matched clauses but split by the introduction of 1:1C-5, 1:6C-L. The common theme is types of gatherings of water, and the formulary trait, internal to the set, is carefully matched items in a list.

Niddah: None.

Makhshirin: None.

Zabim

6. See iii 110, 111.

Tebul Yom: None.

Yadayim

6. 3:3-5, 4:5: This clearly forms a subdivision on Scriptures which impart uncleanness of hands, stated in simple declarative sentences. The on-that-day-group, 4:1-4, interrupts.

Uqsin

7. 2:2A + 2:4A: this matched couplet has been split up by interpolated materials.
See iii 120.

8. 3:1-3 + 9: See iii 123.

viii. The Construction of the Mishnah's Intermediate Divisions: General Traits

Apart from the grouping of cognitive units in accord with theme and formulary or formal traits, there is one further aspect of the subdivision which has repeatedly come to the fore. This is the pronounced tendency of the intermediate division to be formed in aggregations of three and multiples of three, or five and multiples of five, cognitive units. The following catalogues go over the ground of sections ii-vii and enumerate components of 190 intermediate divisions. (The reason that the number exceeds the 167 divisions of sections ii-vi is that, for internal reasons, a few intermediate divisions produce entries on more than one of the following catalogues.) The result is as follows:

Threes and multiples of three	91	48%
Fives and multiples of five	73	38%
Other	26	14%
	190	100%

Since in any random sequence, one third of the numbers will be multiples of three, and one fifth, equivalently, multiples of five, these are noteworthy disproportions. I have stressed that one may count the components of the subdivisions in more than one way, so that others, examining the same subdivisions, may produce different statistics. I am inclined, nonetheless, to think it probable, though not proved, that in the organization of intermediate divisions, the redactors paid considerable attention to the number of cognitive units strung together therein and tended to arrange matters so that sequences of threes and fives would characterize their organization of materials.

1.   Threes and multiples of three

    1.   ii 1
    2.   ii 3 (17:1-3)
    3.   ii 3 (17:11-12)
    4.   ii 6
    5.   ii 7
    6.   ii 8 (three basic entries)
    7.   ii 9 (9)
    8.   ii 10 (6)
    9.   ii 12 (6)
    10.   ii 13 (3)
    11.   ii 14 (3)
    12.   ii 17 (9)
    13.   ii 21 (6)
    14.   ii 22 (6)

15. iii 1 (3)
16. iii 2 (9)
17. iii 4 (3)
18. iii 5 (3)
19. iii 8 (3)
20. iii 9 (21)
21. iii 10 (12)
22. iii 11 (27)
23. iii 12 (6)
24. iii 18 (6)
25. iii 20 (12)
26. iii 22 (6)
27. iii 25 (3)
28. iii 27 (9)
29. iii 28 (3)
30. iii 29 (3)
31. iii 30 (21)
32. iii 31 (6 -- if understood)
33. iii 33 (12)
34. iii 36 (6)
35. iii 37 (3)
36. iii 38
[37. iii 40 (60)]
[38. iii 41 (30)]
39. iii 42 (18 + 1 to conclude,
    compare M. Kel. 24:1-15 + 16)
[40. iii 43 (15)]
41. iii 44 (3)
42. iii 45 (3)
43. iii 50 (45)
44. iii 51 (60)
(45. iii 52 [3 disputes,
    3 glosses]
46. iii 53 (sets of 3)
47. iii 57 (6)
48. iii 58 (3)
49. iii 61 (39)
50. iii 65 (3)
51. iii 69 (12)
52. iii 70 (3)
53. iii 72 (6)
54. iii 74 (18)

55.   iii 77 (3)
56.   iii 79 (3)
58.   iii 81 (9)
59.   iii 85 (3)
60.   iii 86 (3)
61.   iii 87 (3)
62.   iii 88 (3)
63.   iii 90 (27)
64.   iii 93 (9)
65.   iii 95 (3)
66.   iii 96 (6)
67.   iii 97 (12)
68.   iii 99 (6)
69.   iii 100 (3)
70.   iii 101 (6)
71.   iii 104 (3)
72.   iii 107 (3)
73.   iii 109 (3)
74.   iii 111 (3)
75.   iii 112 (15/3)
76.   iii 113 (3)
77.   iii 114 (3)
78.   iii 118 (9)
79.   iii 119 (9)
80.   iii 120 (12)
81.   iii 122 (6)
82.   iii 125 (3)
83.   iv 2 (12)
84.   iv 5 (6)
85.   v 2 (3/12)
86.   v 4 (3)
87.   v 5 (6)
88.   v 6 (3)
89.   vi 3 (33)
90.   vi 5 (3)
91.   vii 5 (6)

2.   Fives and multiples of five
     1.   ii 4
     2.   ii 5 (15)
     3.   ii 15 (20)
     4.   ii 16 (20)

5.   ii 24 (5 +)
6.   iii 3 (5)
7.   iii 6 (5)
8.   iii 7 (5)
9.   iii 13 (5)
10. iii 15 (5 disputes)
11. iii 17 (15)
12. iii 19 (5)
13. iii 21 (40)
14. iii 23 (5)
15. iii 24 (5)
16. iii 26 (10)
17. iii 28 (5)
18. iii 32 (5)
19. iii 34 (10)
20. iii 35 (5)
21. iii 38 (5)
22. iii 40 (60)
23. iii 41 (30)
24. iii 43 (15)
25. iii 44 (5 + 15)
26. iii 47 (5)
27. iii 49 (5)
28. iii 51 (60)
29. iii 52 (55) [Compare List 1,
     No. 45.]
30. iii 54 (20)
31. iii 55 (40)
32. iii 56 (20)
33. iii 60 (25)
34. iii 62 (15)
35. iii 63 (15)
36. iii 64 (40)
37. iii 67 (15)
38. iii 68 (15)
39. iii 71 (15)
40. iii 72 (5)
41. iii 73 (10)
42. iii 75 (5/15)
43. iii 76 (10)
44. iii 78 (10)
45. iii 83 (10)

46.   iii 84 (30)
47.   iii 91 (25)
48.   iii 92 (20)
49.   iii 94 (5)
50.   iii 98 (10/70)
51.   iii 102 (20)
52.   iii 103 (15)
53.   iii 105 (5)
54.   iii 106 (5)
55.   iii 108 (10)
56.   iii 110 (5)
57.   iii 111 (5)
[58.   iii 112 (15)]
59.   iii 115 (20)
60.   iii 116 (35)
61.   iii 121 (5)
62.   iii 123 (5, including 3:9)
63.   iii 124 (10)
64.   iv 1 (5)
65.   iv 3 (10)
66.   iv 4 (5)
67.   iv 11 (50)
68.   v 1 (5)
69.   v 3 (10)
70.   v 4 (5)
71.   v 11 (50)
72.   vi 2 (20)
73.   vii 3 (15)

3.   Other
1.   ii 2 (2)
2.   ii 34 (7)
3.   ii 13 (4)
4.   iii 54 (8)
5.   iii 14 (4 + 2)
6.   iii 15 (8)
7.   iii 16 -- no clear pattern
8.   iii 59 (7)
9.   iii 66 (4)
10.   iii 78 (10:8 -- 7)
11.   iii 82 (7)
12.   iii 89 (4)

13. iii 117 (4)
14. iv 12 (11)
15. v 1 -- no clear pattern
16. v 3 -- no clear pattern
17. v 7 -- no clear pattern
18. v 8 -- no clear pattern
19. v 12 -- no clear pattern
20. v 13 -- no clear pattern
21. v 1 -- no clear pattern
22. vi 5 (4)
23. vi 7 (2)
24. vii 1 (4)
25. vii 6 (4)
26. vii 7 (2)

ix. Conclusion

Even though the sustained and consistent application of the stated logical criteria may produce results different from those presented here, particularly in section iii, the proposed conclusion will stand firm. There can be no doubt whatsoever that the systematic demarcation of the Mishnah's principal divisions, the tractates, into intermediate divisions ("chapters") is demanded by the Mishnah's internal evidence. Shifts in distinctive theme coincide with shifts in formulary pattern. Some of the patterns, to be sure, are more striking than others. "Simple declarative sentences" are hardly comparable in aesthetic and mnemonic effect to apocopation, mild or extreme. The fact remains, nonetheless, that we are able decisively to show pronounced effort at organizing materials in such a way that grammatical and syntactical distinctions accompany the movement from one thematic, conceptual, or other intellectual intermediate division of a tractate to the next. Furthermore, it seems evident, though the evidence by no means can be regarded as probative, that the organizers attempted to group materials by sequences of threes or fives.

CHAPTER THREE

THE PROTASIS

2. THE MISHNAH'S SMALLEST COMPONENTS

COGNITIVE UNITS AND THEIR MNEMONIC FORMULATION

i. Definitions

The Mishnah's internal evidence reveals that primary to the organization and redaction of the document are principal divisions, tractates, and intermediate divisions, "chapters." It also is clear from the earlier inquiries that these intermediate divisions are composed of still smaller units, which are now to be defined.

These units to begin with are distinguished from one another by the same criteria as separate one intermediate unit from another, namely, both thematic and formal traits. Sentences or small groups of sentences, exhibiting recurrent traits of stereotype formulation, cover a single problem, issue, or principle, supply opinions assigned to a single authority, or in some other way convey a single rule, idea, or thought on a given subject. Each such unit of thought -- hence, cognitive unit or "smallest whole unit of discourse" -- is the result of careful formulation. Each one, moreover, represents the formal result of a single cogent process of cognition, that is, analysis of a situation and statement of a rule pertaining to it, observation of a recurrent phenomenon and provision of a generalization covering all observations, reflection upon basic rules and their generation of, or application to, secondary and tertiary details or situations -- in all, again, the product of an act of thought. The definition of the Mishnah's smallest whole and irreducible literary-conceptual units as the end-result of an act of thought proceeds along lines by now familiar. We specify distinctive literary forms and formulary patterns and isolate their occurrences, then examine the ways in which said forms and patterns contain and convey whole, complete, and irreducible ideas, rules, opinions -- the results of a single sequence of cognition on a single matter.

The Mishnah's language is like ours in morphology and syntax, with a verb which produces statements of past-completed, present-continuing, and future action in both indicative and subjunctive moods, a sentence-structure which normally consists of subject and predicate, and a reasonably full repertoire of devices by which ideas may be expressed in ways fundamentally the same as those by which we convey ideas. That is why we can translate the Mishnah in a literal, word-for-word way and thereby produce in English or German a clear sense of the order and meaning of the Hebrew words. That also is why we cannot take for granted the far from random, and far from broad, range of formal-linguistic possibilities explored by the formulators of the Mishnah. In fact they express their ideas in accord with a remarkably limited repertoire of forms and formulary patterns. Forms, words which function in, but bear no meaning distinctive to, a particular cognitive unit, and formulary patterns, grammatical arrangements of words distinctive to their subject but in fixed syntactical patterns serviceable for a wide range of subjects, are remarkable for their discipline. Outside of the dialogue in stories and narratives (which are rare in the Mishnah), formalization and stereotype patterns of language characterize the whole of the Mishnah. Whatever ideas people had therefore are shaped to conform to a readily discerned set of literary conventions, grammatical patterns applicable to thoughts on any subject and accessible to all of the Mishnah's themes. We already have noticed, for example, that the eleven themes of our Order's twelve principal divisions produce exactly the same sorts of intermediate divisions, to be analyzed and dissected in accord with a single limited literary-thematic (not solely thematic) criterion. The same observation derives from the examination of the thousands of individual cognitive units. The Mishnah is a public and anonymous corpus, in which the contribution of individuals is limited to formalized expression of distinctive conceptions, and which entirely excludes particular ways of stating said conceptions. All cognitive units are forced to conform to a severely limited range of conventions of formulation and form.

Our task is in two parts. First, in section ii, we take up the task of the analysis of the diverse but disciplined range of patterns of declarative sentences. Second, in section iii, we ask about the relationship between the formulation of the cognitive units and their redaction into conglomerates of such units, intermediate divisions, that is, the relationship between tradental and redactional formulation and formalization.

ii. Formulary Patterns in the Mishnah: The Declarative Sentence

Our taxonomy of declarative sentences is based upon differentiation of gross and general syntactical traits, characteristic of cognitive units on any subject. Our interest at present is not in how one syntactical phenomenon may differ from another phenomenon of the same basic sort, e.g., two sentences, both having a subject, a closely joined verb, and a smoothly-attached predicate. We list together all cognitive units, the distinctive formulary characteristic of which is simply a smooth flow from subject through predicate. These then are distinguished from cognitive units in which the subject is disjoined from the predicate, in which the subject itself is complex, or in which distinctive formulary traits consistently characterize the predicate. Our purpose thus is to ask whether, in fact, the omnipresent, declarative sentences are as a whole differentiable in terms of recurrent syntactical patterns. Only later on shall we inquire into the ways in which sentences of a given pattern -- the "simple declarative sentence" -- may be distinguished from one another. This itself is solely in the context of the intermediate redactional unit, at which point such distinctions exhibit functional significance for the solution of the Mishnah's formal-redactional problem.

In the several lists, the opening items are spelled out in detail, to provide a clear example of the sort of formulary pattern under discussion. Thereafter references grow somewhat briefer. The entries bear the following markings: [] = minor example; * = dispute; and # = sizable collection of examples.

In order to spell out the character and distribution of declarative sentences of various sorts, I have taken each stich of the apodosis of a dispute and treated it as if it were a complete sentence. I thus add the protasis to one of the two (or more) stichs of the apodosis. Since we already know that the attributive, <u>X says</u>, is a form independent of what is expressed and external to the formulary pattern in which it appears, I delete the attributive:

A chicken which is cooked for two hours (<u>the House of Shammai say</u>) is uncooked.

This procedure allows us to see the traits of the several cognitive units which, in theory, serve as primary components of the dispute. It further shows us how the dispute's composite character preserves the syntactical traits of its (prior) units and how such traits conform to their tradental-redactional setting.

The decisive formulary traits occur in the protasis, that is, the opening element of a cognitive unit. They may or may not continue throughout the unit. In apocopation, for example, we find the striking disjunctures of components of the subject in particular at the inaugural sentence of a cognitive unit, while declarative sentences may follow until the problem and solution of the unit have been expressed. The differentiating formulary characteristics are thus to be discovered in the commencement of the unit. These traits will be revealed, in that opening sentence, either in the subject or in the predicate. The decisive differentiation is exhibited in the connection -- the interface -- between the subject and the predicate.

One sort of sentence flows smoothly from subject to verb to complement or predicate. The verb refers to the subject and is completed at the complement or predicate. This sort of sentence is characterized as the simple declarative sentence (List 1).

In another sort, the subject of the sentence is duplicated, but then leads directly into the predicate. Sometimes this is effected through a shift in word-order, e.g., <u>chickens -- when are they fully cooked in the pot?</u> That is, the topic, chickens, is placed before the interrogative, <u>when</u>. This pattern (List 2) would not seem peculiar at all, were it not for the numerous instances in which the word-order yields nothing like the duplicated protasis, e.g., <u>A chicken which is cooked for three hours is fully boiled</u>.

There is only one construction in which the formulary peculiarity is exhibited in the apodosis, and this is the contrastive complex, in which we have clearcut balance between the predicate of one sentence, normally a brief one, and that which follows, e.g., <u>X/unclean, Y/clean</u> (List 3).

Two further complex constructions complete our taxonomy, both of them exhibiting apocopation, the one mild, the other severe, and both affecting the subject of the sentence or its protasis (in the case of the latter). What is cut off, or apocopated, is the subject of the sentence, which is disconnected from the verb of the same sentence. When we have a complete disjuncture between the opening unit(s) and the predicate, so that the latter refers to, and depends upon, nothing in the former, then we have the extreme apocopation which is so striking a formulary pattern in our order.

Mild apocopation, by contrast, normally begins <u>he who</u> (or, <u>that which</u>), and the predicate, while not referring to the subject of <u>he who/that which</u>, does join up to an element of the inaugural clause, e.g., to the implied or stated object of <u>he who</u> or <u>that which</u>, or to the consequence of what <u>he who does</u> has done (List 4).

The extreme apocopation, as I said, is made extreme because none of the stichs are the subject of the sentence, and they may be many or few, refers to the predicate (List 5).

These definitions of formulary patterns exhaust the large-scale categories of syntactical-grammatical types among which all declarative sentences may be divided. I have omitted two sorts of constructions. First is the list, whose distinctive traits require no discussion. A second exception is the major unit in balanced declarative sentences (= #). Entries on the list of intermediate units built out of sentences exhibiting internally-unitary formulary traits (with or without a common theme) are not discussed below; many of them are not included at all, because these sentences too exhibit such distinctive traits as not to require further specification.

I. The Simple Declarative Sentence: Subject + Verb + Predicate

In these sentences, which may or may not contain an implied <u>if</u>, all smoothly flows from the subject through the verb to the predicate. This of course constitutes by far the largest group, for we should achieve nothing by imposing non-syntactical, therefore impressionistic, criteria of differentiation, e.g., by distinguishing long from short sentences, sentences with subordinate clauses from those lacking them, and the like. Later on (section iv), we shall ask whether declarative sentences of the simple sort themselves may be differentiated, not in form but in <u>provenance</u> and <u>function</u>. That is, are we able to show that one thematic subdivision, hitherto described merely as characterized by the formulary constituted by the simple declarative sentence, exhibits sentence-patterns different from those of some other thematic subdivision, also characterized as distinguished by its use of the simple declarative sentence? To investigate that sort of differentiation among simple sentences outside of the framework of the already-designated intermediate divisions would serve no useful and practical purpose, since it would answer no important question.

Kelim

1. 2:3P: This is the general rule: Whatever among clay utensils has no inside has no outside.

2. 3:2L: Lamp the mouth of which is removed is clean, and one of ... the mouth of which ... is clean.

3. 3:7C-D (+E): A pot which was perforated and repaired with pitch (Yosé declares) is clean, because ... +E, +F.

* 4. 3:8D-H: A funnel of wood ... which one stopped up (Eleazar b. ^{C}Azariah declares) is unclean (^{C}Aqiva declares) is unclean, clean; (Yosé) clean.

* 5. 4:1A-C+D: A sherd which cannot ... because of its ear, or on which there was a point and which the point overbalances is clean. [If] the handle-piece was removed ..., it is clean. (Judah declares) it is unclean. D: A jar -- which was diminished but which ... (Judah declares) is unclean. (Sages declare) is clean.

6. 4:2, 3A-B: A jar which was ... is clean. A spoiled jar which ... even though ... is clean, because ... 3A-B: What is ...? Any whose ...

7. 4:3D+E, F, G: [If] there were in it extruding points, any part which ... is unclean by ..., etc. [The implied if does not produce any sort of apocopation or duplicated subject (Lists 2, 4).]

* 8. 5:3A, B, C, D, E: A crown is clean. The fender, when it is ..., receives ... If one joined it ..., even ..., it is unclean. Three items + which are on ... receive uncleanness by contact, not airspace, words of Meir (Simeon declares) they are clean.

9. 5:4A (+ ma^caseh): An oven which ... or which ... or which ... is unclean.

10. 5:5A-C: Chimney piece of ... is clean, and that of .. is unclean, because ... C: Rim of ... is unclean, that of dyers is clean.

11. 5:6A-B: An oven which one filled ... from the top ... is unclean through contact, from ... is unclean through ... C-D+E: [If] one set it and put ... there (Judah says), if one heats and it ..., it is unclean. Despite the length and complexity of C-D+E, in fact we have a simple sentence, in which the predicate carries through and refers to the subject. The contrast is to 4:4A-D, List 4, No. 6: A clay vessel which has ... rims, if the innermost Primp ... all [rims] are clean, etc. There [rims] does not refer to clay vessel, while here (A-B) unclean does refer to oven.

12. 5:7A, B, C, D, E, F: An oven which was made unclean -- how do they clean it? This is not apocopation of any sort, simply an idiomatic word-order, which places the predicate before the subject. I see no duplicated subject, by contrast to the items of List 2. The remainder of the unit consists of standard declarative sentences, subject, verb, complement.

13. 5:8A, B, C: [If] one divided it ..., it is clean. [If] one plastered ..., it receives uncleanness ... [If] one separated ... and put ... (concerning this one did they say ... and it) is clean.

14. 5:9A-B, C, D: The category to which this item belongs is unclear. If we read the pericope as presently printed, we have: An oven which ... and one which one made ... and on which one placed ... and which is clean [if] it was made unclean and one removed ... is clean. [If] one restored ..., it is clean, etc. Accordingly, we seem to have a long but uncomplicated sentence. C and D, with an understood if, continue the same matter.

* 15. 5:10A-C: [If] one cut it up and put ..., (Eliezer says) it is clean. Sages, unclean.

16. 5:11A, B, C, D: An oven made of stone or metal is clean, and it is unclean on account of ... [If] it was, [and] one made for it, it is .., etc. These are standard simple declarative sentences, in which the predicate refers to the subject of the opening clause.

17. 7:1A-B, C, D-E, F,G: A fire-basket which ..., is unclean, because ... + further declarative sentences.

18. 7:2: An ashbox which has ... is clean as ..., and unclean as ... [As to] its sides, that which ... Its wide side (Meir declares) is clean, etc.

19. 7:3A, B, C, D, E, F + G-H: A double-stove which was divided ... is clean/unclean, etc.

20. 7:4A-B, C, D, E-G: [If] it was separated ... when it is ..., it is unclean through ..., less is clean, etc.

21. 7:5A (B), C (D), E (F), G-I: [If] one of them was ..., they are susceptible, etc.

22. 7:6: How do they measure? One places, etc.

*   23. 8:8A + B, C; D, E, F: [If] it is found ..., (Judah says), [space] from the rim ... is clean. This set continues the issue of 8:7, but does so in uncomplicated declarative sentences, as is commonly the case in pericopae inaugurated by apocopation.

24. 8:9A-B, D; D-F+G, H: An earth-oven which has ... is unclean, etc.

\#   25. 9:6D-G, H-I, J-K, L-M: The spindle which ... etc., [if] they entered are made unclean.

26. 10:3A + B or C (+ D-H): A plug of a jar which became loosened but has not fallen out (Judah says) affords protection, etc.

*   27. 10:4A-C (D-E): A ball or coil which one placed, if one plastered ..., does not afford ...

28. 10:5: A jar which was sealed off but whose pitch stands, etc. (Judah says) afford protection.

Note that Nos. 26-28 continue lists, which themselves are formed by simple declarative sentences.

29. 10:6G-I, J, K-L: A board which is placed, if one plastered, affords protection.

30. 12:2G: This is the general rule ...

31. 12:6: Four things Gamaliel declares unclean and sages clean, etc.

32. 12:7A, B, C: A denar which became defective and which one fashioned ... is unclean, etc.

\#   33. 13:2A-B, C, D, E(+F-G): A fork whose shovel end was removed in uncleanness because of its tooth. [If] its tooth was removed, it is unclean because of its shovel end. 4X.

34. 13:3B (A, C): As above.

*   35. 13:4B (vs. B): As above.

\#   36. 13:7A, B, C: Irons broken, etc. -- lo, these are unclean. B: 4 items + lo, these are unclean. + Joshua.

*   37. 14:2A (+B), C, D, E, F-H: A staff on the head of which one made ... is unclean, etc.

38. 14:3A, B, C, D, E, F, G: Crowbar of ... and pick of ..., lo, these are unclean, etc. Sequence of random simple declarative sentences.

39. 14:7A, B, D, E: Dispute composed of complete sentences.

*   40. 14:8A, B, C, D (major unit of 3 balanced sentences), E, F: Declarative sentences, Except for D, they appear random.

*\#   41. 15:1F-K, L-R+S: Two long, smooth, carefully balanced sentences, with extensive subordinate clauses.

*\#   42. 15:4A, B (+C: This is the general rule): All ... are unclean, except ... All are clean, except ...

\#   43. 15:5A, B: Exactly as above. Nos. 42-3 form a major unit of balanced sentences.

* 44. 16:1A-B: Every wooden utensil which has been divided is clean, except ...

*# 45. 17:2B, C, D + E: If it does not ..., even though it ..., it is unclean (3X).

#* 46. 17:4A (+B-C, D, E-F), 17:5A (+B-F), 17:6A (+B-C), 17:7A (+B), 17:8A-B, C-D, E-F (+G-I), 17:9A (+B, C-D, + 17:10): X of which they have spoken is/are ... The inserted materials clearly break up a single major, balanced construction of declarative sentences.

#* 47. 17:11A: And there are instances in which they have spoken +17:11B: Measures for wet and dry -- their measure is ... (+C, D-K). 17:12A: And there are instances ... a ladleful ... [if] according to ..., etc.

48. 17:13A-B: All ... are clean, except ...

#* 49. 17:14A, B, C, D-E + F, G: And there is uncleanness for that created on first day. Second, none, etc.

* 50. 18:1: The chest -- (the House of Shammai say) is measured from the inside, (House of Hillel say) is measured from the outside. +D, E.

#* 51. 18:2A + B/C, D/E (+F-H): Its device, when it may be slipped of +4 rules which complete the subject of the sentence, balanced phrase for phrase.

* 52. 18:3A-C + D, E; F: Chest, box, etc., one of whose legs has been removed, even though ..., are clean, because ...

* 53. 18:4: A bed frame which one set ... (Meir + Judah declare) is unclean, etc.

*# 54. 18:5A-C + D-E-F+G-H: A bed which was ... [if] ..., is unclean. [If] ..., it is clean. [If] one cut ..., it is clean. +18:6A-C, D-E, 18:7A-B, C, D, E, F, G + H, (interruption: 18:8), 18:9A, B, C-D: These entries continue the opening pattern of fully spelled out, major constructions, lacking only if.

* 55. 19:4A, C-D: [If] a Zab was carried on the bed and bedgirth, etc.

56. 19:7A (+B, C, D with if understood at B, C): A box whose opening is on top is susceptible, etc.

57. 19:8A: As above.

* 58. 19:9A (+B, C, D-F+G): A box which was damaged on its side is susceptible ...

59. 19:10: A dung basket which was damaged (Meir declares) is unclean, etc.

60. 20:2A, B-C, E, F-G, H-K (major unit of balanced sentences): A bag-pipe is insusceptible to midras, etc.

61. 20:3A, B-C + D, E + F-H: A staff which one made ... is a connector for uncleanness, etc.

* 62. 20:4A-C + D, E: A large trough which was damaged and which one adapted (Aqiba declares) is unclean, sages, clean until ...

63. 20:5A-C, D-F, G-H: As above.

* 64. 20:6A + B-E: As above.

* 65. 20:7A + B, C, D-E: As above.

*# 66. 21:1A, B, C, D, 22A, B, C (+D), 21:3A, B (+C), D (+E-F): He who touches ... is clean/unclean.

#* 67. 22:1A-C + D: The table and side-table which were damaged ... are unclean.

* 68. 22:2A-C: The table, one of the legs of which was removed, is clean. [If] ..., it is clean. [If] ..., it is unclean.

69. 22:3A-C: As above.

*   70. 22:4A-D, E-H: A chair of which ... removed (the House of Shammai declare) is unclean.

71. 22:5: As above.

*   72. 22:6A, B, C: As above.

*   73. 22:7A-C + D: As above.

74. 22:8A + B-D, E: A chest, the top of which ... is unclean because of the bottom, and vice versa.

*   75. 22:9A-C, D, E: As above.

N.B. Nos. 67-75 follow a single pattern, slightly varied at 74.

*   76. 22:10A-B, C-D, E, F-H + I, J, K: A toilet is susceptible to midras and corpse-uncleanness, etc.

77. 23:3A-B + C, D: What is the difference ...?

78. 24:1-15 + 16 (17): There are three kinds of, etc.

*#   79. 25:1-5, 7-9: All utensils have, etc. Simple declarative sentences throughout, which disputes in each pericope, except 25:6. 25:6 breaks the pattern, see List 4, No. 28.

*#   80. 26:4A-D (+E-M): A sandal, one of whose straps ..., is subject to midras, etc.

N.B.: Follows the pattern of No. 54, making the same point as that set.

*   81. 26:6A, B-D, E + F-G: A leather bag ... is subject to midras, etc.

82. 26:7: Balanced, fully spelled out, simple sentences.

83. 26:8: As above.

*   84. 27:5A-C (+D-I): Worn-out pieces which one ... (^CAqiba declares) are unclean, etc.

*   85. 27:9: A sheet which ... is ... but is ...

N.B.: 27:9 is integral to the 3 X 3 construction, listed above. This construction is omitted here.

*   86. 28:4A, B, C: Wrappers, whether ... or whether ..., are unclean, etc.

87. 28:5A, B, C, D: Long but simple declarative sentences.

88. 28:9A, B, C, D: The pad ... is susceptible ...

89. 28:10 A-B, C, D, E: Simple sentences.

*   90. 30:2A-B, C-D, E-G: A mirror is clean, and a tray ... is unclean, etc.

91. 30:3A-B, C, D, E: A glass cup, the greater part of which ..., is clean, etc.

92. 30:4A-B, C, D, E: Simple sentences (See List 3, No. 68.)

Ohalot

93. 2:2A-B, C-E, F-H (I-K), L-M, N: A quarter-<u>log</u> from one corpse [render unclean ...]. ^CAqiva: From two corpses. The opinions in each dispute depend on the apodosis of A. I-K are on List 2, No. 24.

94. 2:6A + C or C: 6 Items + (^CAqiva declares) are unclean, etc.

95. 2:7A + B or C + (D), E + F or G, H + I-J: As above.

96. 3:1A-C, D, E, F-G, H, I, J: He who (Dosa declares) is clean. (Sages declare) is unclean.

97. 3:3A-B (+ C-E): [If] it was poured out, if its place was ... and one overshadowed ..., he is clean.

98. 3:5A + B, C, D-E[F-G (apocopated)], H, J: What is ...? +Answers.

[99. 5:5A, B + C, D: [If] they were ..., the whole is clean. Continues 5:4, List 4, No. 36.]

100. 6:5A-B, C-D: [If] uncleanness is, and beneath it is ..., if there is ..., all is unclean. If there is not ..., they regarded ...

* 101. 6:7A-B: Utensils which are ... are clean, etc.

102. 7:1A-B: [If] Uncleanness is in the wall ..., all the upper rooms ... are unclean.

* 103. 7:3A, B, C + D-E, F: [If] the corpse is in the house and in it are many ..., they are all unclean, etc.

* 104. 11:3A, B, C: A thick cloak and ... do not bring ... [If] a man was placed + Houses + he does not, etc.

* 106. 11:7: Complete declarative sentences, in a dispute.

107. 11:9A, B, C, D: Utensils which are ... are clean. [If] uncleanness is ..., the house is ..., etc.

* 108. 12:8A: [If] ... is attached, (Eliezer declares) the house is clean, etc. +B-C, D, E.

109. 14:1A, B, C, D, E: The wall projection brings uncleanness, whatever its depth.

110. 14:2A, B-C: As above.

111. 14:3A, B: As above.

112. 15:1A, B, D: A thick cloak, etc., do not ... Tablets ... do not ..., and if they were ...

*# 113. 16:2-18:10 [excluding 17:4, 18:2, List 4, Nos. 42-43]: This entire set consists of simple declarative sentences, subject, verb, complement.

Negaim

*# 114. 2:1-3:2: As above, see #113.

115. 4:1-3: As above, see #113.

116. 6:8K-L + [If] + M, N-P, 7:1: Sequence of simple sentences, with <u>if</u> understood.

117. 7:2: [If] their color changed, etc.

* 118. 7:4A, B-D, E-K: He who removes ... transgresses ...

* 119. 7:5A: He on whom was, and it was ..., is clean. [If] he intentionally ...

120. 8:1A, B-C + D, E-F: With an understood <u>if</u> at B, D, E, we have simple declarative sentences.

121. 8:4A-C, D-F + G-H: All ... when they ... are ..., etc.

122. 8:8A-B-C, D, E, F: [If] it broke forth ..., during ..., he is unclean.

123. 8:10A; There is a man who ... C-E: he who was ..., and the tokens went away, [if] he did not ..., is clean. Duplicated: 8:10F-K, but G-I + J are apocopated. (See List 5, No. 69).

124. 9:1A, B-C + D, E-G, 9:2A, B, C, D, E, F, G: Simple declarative sentences on the boil and burning. + Colloquy, 9:3.

125. 10:1-4: Simple declarative sentences on the scall.

126. 10:8: He on whom was ... is unclean. [If] black hair ... he is clean.

127. 10:9A, B, C + D, E-F + G: As above.

128. 10:10: Follows the exact pattern of 9:1, 10:1.

130. 11:1A-B, E, F-J: All garments are susceptible ... except of gentiles, etc.

* 131. 11:3A-B + C, D, E: Complete declarative sentences, forming a dispute.

* 132. 11:4D-I: Garments are made unclean by ...

133. 11:6A-B, C-D: [If] a plague ..., it affords ...

* 134. 11:8A, D-I: The warp and woof are subject ... forthwith, etc.

135. 11:10A-B, C, D, E: [If] it appeared on ... the web is clean, etc.

136. 11:11A-E: Whatever is ... is ..., for example ... (+ 5 items + C-D) -- lo, these are ...

137. 12:1A, C, D: All houses are ... 5 items + [are] not susceptible ...

138. 12:2A-C, D, E, F: A house, one of the sides of which ... is clean, etc.

* 139. 12:3A-H: How many? + Answers.

* 140. 12:4A-B, C, D-E, F, G: Wood -- sufficient to, etc.

141. 12:5: How is inspection carried out -- smooth declarative sentences.

P142. 13:1: Ten [rules on] plagues in houses + list. See List 4, No. 52.]

143. 13:4A, B, D: A house which ... renders unclean on the inside.

144. 13:5A-C (+G-F): He who builds ... and the plague returned], takes the stone ...

145. 13:7A-B, C-D, E-F + G: [If] the unclean ... he is ...

146. 13:8A, B, C, D: A clean person who ... is made ... (4X).

* 147. 13:10A-C, D-F, G: [If] he was standing ..., but put ...if he remained ..., they are unclean.

*# 148. 13:12D, E: Whatever affords, etc. -- long balanced simple sentences.

*# 149. 14:1A-B, C, D, E, F + G, H, etc: Sequences of simple declarative sentences.

Parah

* 150. 1:1A-B, C, D-E, etc.: (Eliezer says), A heifer [is to be] a year old, etc. When the components of the disputes are spelled out, they form simple declarative sentences throughout.

151. 1:2, 3, 4: As above.

#*   152.   2:1A + B, C + D, F-I, 2:2B-F, 2:3 A, B-C, D-F, G, 2:4, 2:5A-B, C, D-F: Simple declarative sentences.

#*   153.   3:1-11: Simple declarative sentences, forming a narrative.

#*   154.   4:1A-F: A cow which ... is unfit. (Eliezer declares) it is fit. Repeated pattern: H-I, J-K (+ L-M).

155.   4:2-3: [If] one ... it is unfit, at 4:2A, B, C, D, 4:3A, B, C +D.

156.   4:4A, B, C, D-E, F, G, H, I: Rules stated as declarative sentences.

157.   5:1A, B, C, (D-G): He who brings ... spends the night ...

158.   5:2A, B, C: He who ... must dry ...

159.   5:5A, C-D, E-F: With all ... do they mix, etc.

*   160.   5:6A-B, C-E: An egg (Yosé declares) is fit, etc.

*   161.   6:2A-B, C, D-F: [If] the ash was, (Meir and Simeon say), One takes ... and mixes ...

162.   6:4A, B, C: [If] he placed ...,it is unfit, etc.

163.   7:5A-B, C, D, E, F-G: He who draws ... draws first for himself, etc.

#*   164.   8:8A-B, C-D, E-F, 8:9A-C, D-F, G-H, 8:10I-J, K-L + M-P, 8:11R, S, T-U, V, W-X: a series of simple declarative sentences.

165.   9:2A-D, E-F-G, 9:3A-B: [If] cattle ..., it is], C-D, E-F = G-H, 9:4A + B or C: He who forms (Eliezer says) has rendered it ..., etc. + D-H: As above.

#*   166.   9:8A-B, C-D, 9:9E-F: Water which ... renders unclean, etc.

167.   10:1A-C, D-Y; 10:2A, B, C-E, F-H; 10:3A, B-D, E, F-H; 10:4A-C, D-F; 10:5G-I, J-L; 10:6D-E, F-G, H-I, J-K, L, M-N + O-Q: Simple declarative sentences, some with subordinate adjectival clauses, many balanced pairs or triplets.

168.   11:2A, B, C, D-E: As above.

#*   169.   11:4-6: See above.

#*   170.   11:7A, B, C-D, E-F, G, H + I-J; 11:8A-F, 11:9A-B, C, E-K: Simple declarative sentences. See List 2, NO.s 39-40.

171.   12:3A-B, C-D, E-F, G-H (+ I-J): One intended ... and ..., if there is ..., he should not ...

172.   12:5A, B, C-E: The clean person holds ..., and one sprinkles ...

173.   12:10A-C: The cover of ... which is ... (the House of Shammai say) is ... (See List 2, No. 42.)

174.   12:10D-G, 12:11A: [If] he dipped ..., it is ... + B-D, E, F, G.

Tohorot

#*   175.   2:2A: He who eats ... is unclean, etc. + B, 2:3-7 + 8: See above.

*   176.   3:1A-C: The grease and, etc., when they are ..., lo, they are, etc. + D-J, 3:2A + B-C.

177.   3:4A-D, E, F G: Simple declarative sentences.

178.   3:5A, B, C-D: All unclean things [follow] the moment ... if ... etc. Very well balanced units.

179.   3:6A, B: A deaf-mute, etc. -- lo, these are ...

180. 3:7A + B-C: A child who is ... is clean.

181. 3:8A + B/C + D: A child who is (Meir declares) is clean.

* 182 4:5: On account of six ... do they burn ...

183. 4:7-13. See above, No. 140.

184. 5:2: One who said ... (^CAqiva declares) is unclean, etc.

185. 5:8A-D: [If there is] ..., all drops are ...

186. 5:9A-B, C-E, F-H, I-K, L-O: [If] a witness says, etc. With the understood if, all these groups form simple sentences.

* 187. 6:1A, D-H: A place which was ..., when it is, a matter of doubt ...

*# 188. 6:5, 6:6, 6:7, 6:8, 6:9: Sequence of simple declarative sentences.

* 189. 8:7: Outer sides ... (Eliezer says) render ...

* 190. 8:9: A stick which is ..., once one has ..., is ...

#* 191. 9:2A-F, G-I: [If] one has ..., they are ... + 9:3A, B-E + F-K; 9:4A-B: He who completes ... [should give] ... -- smooth sentences.

* 192. 9:7: [If] one wanted ..., let him set ...

193. 9:9A-B, C-N: [If] it was found ..., it is clean.

* 194. 10:4A-D, F-H: He who places ... places with ...

195. 10:8A, B, C, D-E: Simple sentences.

Miqvaot

* 196. 2:4: (Eliezer says), A quarter-qab in the beginning renders ... unfit, and three ... (sages say) Whether in first place or at end, its measure is ...

* 197. 2:5A-E + F-G: A pool which has ..., if it is known ..., is fit, etc.

#* 198. 2:7A-D + E, F-H, 2:8A-C + D, 2:9: He who leaves ... and they filled ... if it is ... if there is ..., breaks them, etc. While the sentence is strung out in several clauses, it nonetheless links protasis to apodosis.

#* 199. 3:1A-F, G-K, L, M-O, P; 3:2A + B-E + F + G-H: 3:3A-D: (Yosé says) Two pools which do not ..., and into this one fell ..., and then which were mingled ... are fit, because ..., etc. The whole construction is smooth.

200. 5:1A, B-D, E-F, G-H: Spring which one ... is unfit, etc.

* 201. 5:2A + B/C-D: [If] one passed ... (Judah says) lo, it is as it was, etc.

202. 5:3A-C, D-F: A spring which ..., if one added ..., lo, it is as it was ...

* 203. 5:4: See above, No. 164.

204. 5:5A-B, C: Flowing water is like a spring, etc.

205. 5:6D-E, F, G+H, I, J: [In] any place in which ... do they dip and dunk, etc.

206. 6:1A: Any [pool] is [valid] as ...

207. 6:4A-C + D: Sponge and bucket which contained ... and fell ... have not spoiled ...

208. 6:7A-C, D-F (+G-J): Intermingling of pools is through a hole ...

* 209. 6:8A-C, D + E-G + H, I-L; 6:10A-E, F, G: They clean pools, higher by lower, etc.

#*   210. 7:3A, B-C, D-E, F-G, H-J; 7:4A-C, 7:5A-E, F-J + K: [If] one rinsed ..., it is valid, etc. A sequence of simple declarative sentences.

*   211. 8:1A, B-C, D-E, F, G-I: Land ... is clean, and its pools are clean, etc.

      212. 8:5A-B, C: A menstruating woman who ... is clean ...

      213. 10:1A-D, E-F, G-H, I, J, K, L; 10:2A, B, C: Simple declarative sentences throughout.

*#   214. 10:6A, B, C-E, F; 10:7A, B, C-D; 10:8A-C, D-E, F-G, H-I, J: Simple declarative sentences, sometimes with if understood.

Niddah

      215. 1:2A + B-E: (How ...) [If] she was ..., she is ...

*   216. 1:4F-F, G-H, I-J, K-M: Who is ...? Any ...

*   217. 1:5N-O, P, Q: As above.

      218. 1:6A-B, C, D: As above.

*   219. 1:7A-C, D-F, G-I, J-K: Even though ..., she must ..., except ..., etc.

*   220. 2:1A, D-E; 2:2A, B, C; 2:3D-E, F, G-H; 2:4A, B, C-D, E; 2:5A-B, C, D: Diverse declarative sentences.

*#   221. 3:1-7: She who produces + verb tied to subject -- long unitary construction.

#*   222. 4:1A, B-D, E; 4:2A-C, 4:3A-B + C-H (House of Shammai declare, is clean, etc), 4:4A, B-D (+ E), F, 4:5: Sequence of simple declarative sentences.

*   223. 4:7A, B-F, G, H-I, J-L: Simple sentences.

*   224. 5:3-6: See above, No. 223.

*   225. 5:7-8: Sages have made parable, etc.

*   226. 5:9A-B, C, D-E, F-G, H, I-J: A girl who ... Let her bring, etc ...

#*   227. 6:1 + 2-10: Above.

*   228. 6:11A-B, C, D-F, G, H: A girl who produces ... performs ...

*   229. 6:12: The two hairs [have to be so long] that hair tip ...

*   230. 6:13: She who sees ... lo, she is in ...

      231. 6:14: She who sees on ... lo, these err.

#*   232. 7:1A-B, C-D, E-F, G-I; 7:2A-C, D-H; 7:3A-B, C, D-F; 7:4A, B, D; 7:5A, B, C, D, E: Sequence of simple declarative sentences.

*#   233. 8:1A-C: She who sees ..., if it was near ..., is unclean, and if not near ..., is clean. + D, E, F, G, H, I-J, K-N; 8:2A: And she blames it ...; B-D, E-F, G-J; 8:3 (ma^c aseh), 8:4: As above.

#*   234. 9:1A-C: The woman who was doing ... and who said ... (Meir says), if she is standing, is unclean, etc. + 9:2A-D, 9:3A-B, C-F, G-I; 9:4A-3, Three women who were sleeping, and blood was found ... re all unclean; D, D, E, 9:5F-G, H, I, J, K-O, P-Q: As above.

*#   235. 9:8A, B-C + D, E; 9:9A, B, C-D, E; 9:10F-G, H, I-J, K-L; 9:11A, B: As above.

#*   236. 10:1A-D, E, F, G, H, I-J: A menstruating woman who, lo, (she) is assumed to be ... + 10:3K-N, O, P.

*   237. 10:4A-C, D, E, F: The Zab, etc., impart uncleanness ...

#*   238. 10:6A, B-C, D; 10:7E-F, G, H: At first did they say ... they reverted to rule ...

Makhshirin

239. 2:1A, B, C-E; 2:2A-B: Simple sentences.

*# 240. 3:6J-K + L-N; 3:7/O-P + Q, R-U + V-X: [If] his olives were ... and rain fell ... if he was happy, it is ...

* 241. 4:4A-B + C, D: A jug into which ... (the House of Shammai say) is to be broken. [Compare No. 198, above.]

242. 4:8A-C + D-F: A dish which is ..., and into which ... is unclean ...

* 243. 4:10A-B, C, D, E, F: Pieces of wood on which liquids ... and rains fell, if [rains] were more ..., are insusceptible], etc.

244. 5:5A-B, C, D-F: [If] one stuck ..., [water] is ...

245. 5:7A, B, C: Water which ... is not ..., etc.

246. 5:9A-D: Any ... is ... except ...

*# 247. 6:2D + E-F, G + H; 6:3A-B + C, D-E, F + G (-J): All ... are ... (5X).

* 248. 6:8A, B + C-O: The milk of the woman imparts susceptibility whether ... or not ... but the milk of the beast ..., etc.

Zabim

#* 249. 1:1A-B: He who sees (the House of Shammai say) is like ... + 1:1C, D-I, K-T; 1:2A-B, He who sees (the House of Shammai say) loses ... + 1:2C-L; 1:3: [If] he saw ..., lo, this one ...; 1:4A-F, 1:5A-D, E-H; 1:6A-D, E-H: Joined by the recurrence of R'H, the unit also exhibits striking formulary cogency.

250. 2:1A-E: Simple sentence.

* 251. 2:3A-B, C, D (+ E-F): He who sees ... does not become susceptible ...

#* 252. 3:1A-D, E-N + O: The Zab etc. who ..., even though ..., lo, these are unclean ...; + 3:2; 3:3.

* 253. 4:5A-C, D-F, G-I, 4:6A-B: Ten cloaks ..., if he slept ..., are all unclean, etc.

254. 4:6C-J; More strict ...

* 255. 4:7A-B, C, D-F, G, H-I: [If] he was ...

256. 5:1-3, 4-5, 6-10 + 11, 12: See above.

Tebul Yom

#* 257. 1:3A-E + F, 1:4A-F + G: Various items + are made unclean by the Tebul Yom ... + 1:5A-D, E; 2:1A-B, C-F.

* 258. 2:6A-C, D: A Jar which sunk, and which a Tebul Yom touched ... if he touched ... is deemed connected, etc. + 2:7A-B + C-D.

259. 2:8A-D, E-F; A bubble which ... is made unclean, etc.

* 260. 3:1A, B-C + D-F, G-H: All stalks ... are connected. Produce which was ... (Meir says,) If one holds -- lo (it) is deemed connected, etc.

* 261. 3:3A-B (+ C-D): The streak which formed ... and which ..., if ... is deemed ...

* 262. 3:4A-C + D: Dough which ... is not made unfit ...

263. 4:2A-B: The woman who ... kneads dough, etc.

* 264. 4:5A-B, C-D + E: At first they would rule ... They reverted to rule (2X).

[265. 4:6 = M. Kel. 13:7, above, No. 36.]

Yadayim

#*   266. 1:1A-C + D, E, F, G; 1:2A-B, C, D, E, F; 1:3A-C, D, E-G, H; 1:4A-C, D-F + G; 1:5A-B, C, D, E-F + G; 2:1A-B, C, D-E; 2:2A-B + C, D, E-F + G; 2:3A + B-G (balanced), H, I-J: Simple declarative sentences of various kinds.

#*   267. 3:2A, B-C, D, E; 3:3A, B; 3:4A, B; 3:5A-C, D-F, G, H, I, J, K, L-N, O-R, S; + 4:5: As above.

Uqsin

      [268. 1:1-4, 6: See above.

*   269. 1:5A-B, C-D: All stalks ... are ...

      270. 2:2A, B-C, D: Simple sentences.

#*   271. 2:3A-B, C, D, E; 2:4A + B-E: As above.

272. 2:5D-E, F; 2:6A-B, C, D + E-H: The nuts which ..., lo, (they) are connected, etc.

#*   273. 2:7A-B + C-D; 2:8A-C + D, E, F, G; 2:9A + B-C; 2:10A, B, C + D-F: As above.

      274. 3:1-3 + 9: See above.

#*   275. 3:4A, B + C; 3:5A-C + D; 3:6A + B or C, D + E or F, G + H or I + J; 3:7A-C, D: As above.

#*   276. 3:10: A bee-hive (Eliezer says) lo (it) is like the ground, etc.

2. The Duplicated Subject

      In these sentences, the distinctive formulary pattern occurs in the construction of the subject of the sentence. The predicate is tightly joined to its duplicated subject, e.g., [As to] + subject + restatement of the subject + tightly joined predicate. The secondary, or duplicated, subject refers to the primary one, and both are served by the same verb and predicate.

Kelim

*   1. 2:2A-C, (D), E, F-H: [As to] the smallest [size] of earthenware utensils -- their bottoms ... their measure is ...

      2. 2:7D: [As to] a tray, [if] one ... is made unclean, all of them are not made unclean.

      3. 2:7H: As above.

      4. 3:2A-C: [As to] a jar, its measure (is) + B + substance (3X).

      5. 3:2D-E, F-G, H, I-J + K: As above.

6. 3:3A-B, C: [As to] a jar which was perforated and which ... and which ... if in the place of the pitch there is ..., it [the jar] is unclean, because ... A potsherd which ... and which ... and which ..., even though ..., is clean, because ...

7. 3:4A, B, D: Three exempla as above.

      8. 4:4E (A-C): Clay vessels -- when do they receive ...? When ..., and that is ...

#*   9. 5:1A-C, D-E (+ F + G-H, I): A baking oven -- its beginning is four, and its remnants are four ... Here the duplicated subject is the reference back to oven in the

duplicated subject constituted by its remnants, just as they at No. 8 duplicates vessels.
5:1D-E repeat the formula.

10. 5:2A-B (+ C-D), E, F, G-I (+ J), K: Double-stove -- its beginning is, etc. The ordinary stove, [if] one made it for baking, its measure is, etc. K: Two ovens side by side, one gives to this one a handbreadth, etc.

11. 5:10D-E + F: Cauldrons of ..., which one digs and plasters with clay, if the clay can stand, it [= the clay, not the cauldrons] is unclean, if not clean.

*   12. 9:7A-C: A colander which is placed ..., [If] it was cracked ..., its [the colander's] measure is ... (+ D) + E-F, G; H-J.

13. 9:8A-C, D-E + F, G (H-J, K-Y): As above.

*#   14. 14:1A: Metal utensils -- how much is their measure? + B, C, D, E, F, G, H (+ I-J).

#*   15. 16:1C, D (+ E), F: Wooden utensils -- when do they receive uncleanness? Bed and cot -- when one will have rubbed them, etc.

16. 16:2A + B, C, D: As above.

17. 16:3A, B, C, D, E: As above.

#*   18. 16:4A + B-C, D-E, F-G, H-I: As above.

#*   19. 17:1A, B, C, D, E, F; 17:2A: All utensils ... their measure is ...

20. 17:3A: As above.

21. 19:1B + D (E-F): The rope -- when is it connected to the bed.

22. 20:7H-I: A reed mat -- when does it receive ...?

23. 23:1A-B C, D-E: The ball etc. -- he who touches them is unclean, etc.

Ohalot

24. 2:2I-K: The ash of burned people (Eliezer says) -- measure is ...

25. 3:6A, B (+ C-E): An olive's bulk -- its opening is ...

#*   26. 13:1A, B + C, D, E, F, etc.: He who makes a hole ..., its measure is ..., etc.

27. 13:2A (+ B-C): A window for -- its measure is ...

28. 13:3: As above.

29. 13:4: As above.

Negaim

[30. 11:8B, C: See List 1, No. 134.]

31. 13:2A-C, E-G: The stone which ..., when he takes it out, he takes out ...

32. 13:6A-C + D-E: A house which ..., he who enters the outer house is ...

33. 13:9: He who ... he and they are, so A-C, D (E-G).

Parah

*   34. 5:3A (+ B-E): A pumpkin [which] they mix with it ...

*   35. 5:4A + B or C (+ D, E): A reed which ... he immerses it ...

36. 5:5B: A ship -- they mix with it ...

37. 5:7A-B (vs. C-D, E-K): A trough which is ... they do not draw with it, etc. 5 items vs. C-D, [If] it was ..., they do ...

38. 10:6A-B + C: A pitcher which touched ... [that which contains pitcher] is unclean.

39. 11:8D: Hyssop on which are -- one cuts it up and ...

40. 12:1A (+ B): Hyssop which is -- one makes it suffice ...

41. 12:8 (E) F-G + H, I, J (+ K-M): A spindle used for ... -- one should not sprinkle on the spindle ...

42. 12:9: 7 items + it is a connector for ..., and not for ...

Tohorot

43. 3:2D-E (+ F-H), 3:3A-C (+ D-G), H-J: A clump ... which fell into the oven, and it [= oven] was heated, it [= oven] is ... The apodosis picks up the subordinated element of the protasis, but in no way is apocopated therefrom.

44. 3:6C-D: Whoever lacks ..., a doubt concerning him is ...

45. 3:8E-H (+ L-M): Dough which had ..., and unclean liquids one ..., if there is ..., lo, these [= dough] are clean.

46. 8:6A-C + D (generalization) + E-F: A pigeon which ..., it is ...

* 47. 9:1A-B + C-I: Olives -- from what time do they ...

* 48. 10:3A-C + D-F: Olive-workers etc., once one has brought them ...

49. 10:8F-H + I-J: An implement ... when ..., one dries them off ...

Miqvaot

50. 4:5: See No. 37. above.

51. 6:1A-B, D (+ E-G): 6:2A-B (+ C-E): Holes and clefts ... one dunks in them as they are. A pit ..., they do not dunk in it ...

52. 6:5A-B + C (D-J); 6:6A-C (+ B-L): Box and chest which are in the sea -- they do not dunk in them ..., etc.

* 53. 6:9A (+ B-E): A wall which is ... which is cracked perpendicularly -- (it) joins together. (This may be a simple sentence.)

* 54. 8:5D-E (+ F-G): He who held ... and immersed them, they are unclean.

* 55. 10:5A-B (+ C, D-E, F-G, H): All handles which are ... one immerses them ...

Niddah

#* 56. 1:1A (+ B-F), G (+ H-I); 2:1A (+ B-D): All women -- sufficient for them is their ...

57. 2:1B-C: the deaf-mute ..., if there are ..., they take care of them.

58. 5:1A-B *C, D-G; 5:2 [joined because of principle of linkage -- through Simeon]: That which goes forth -- they do not sit ... on its account.

[59. 6:13-14: See List 1, No. 23-231.]

* 60. 10:1A-B + C (D-J): A girl whose time had not come ..., (House of Shammai say), They give her ...

Makhshirin: None

Zabim

    61. 2:1F: [As to] a _tumtom_ etc., they place on them ... they are ...

    [62. 3:1A-D: See List 1, No. 252.]

Tebul Yom

    63. 2:2A-C (+ D-K): A cooking pot which is full of liquids and which a Tebul Yom touched, if ..., the liquids are unfit but the pot is clean, etc. (+ This rule is more stringent, etc.)

    [64. 3:1B-C, etc.: See List 1, No. 260.]

    65. 4:3A-B + C: A kneading trough which is ... -- they knead in _it_ ... because ...

Yadayim: None

Uqsin

*   66. 2:1A (+ B-D): All olives which one pickled with their leaves -- _they_ [the leaves] are ..., because ...

*   67. 2:2E-F, G-H (+ I-L): A pit, part of which is detached -- that _part_ which is near, etc.

*   68. 3:8A (+ B-D, E-H): Fish -- from what point do _they_ ... (Continued in simple declarative sentences).

*   69. 3:11A + B or C: Honeycombs -- from what point, etc.

3. The Contrastive Complex Predicate

    In this set the predicate will be pointedly constructed to contrast with that of its neighbor and continuator, e.g., X is A, Y is B, thus:

        If a chicken is cooked for three hours, it is edible . But if a turkey is cooked

        for three hours, it is inedible.

I list pericopae in which the distinctive formulary pattern is primary to the formulary distinctiveness of the unit as a whole, but after Ohalot omit all those cognitive units in which the pattern is tangential to what I deem to be the definitive and paramount formulary traits. Otherwise we should have a very long catalogue, most of the entries being in square brackets, of pericopae in which the predicate of a dispute(!) is un-clean/clean and the like.

Kelim

    1. 2:4A: Lantern which has ... is unclean, and which does not have ... is clean.

    2. 2:4B: As above.

    3. 2:4C: As above + gloss, Because ...

    4. 2:5A-B: Three items + clean, and if, unclean. Cover ... when perforated, clean. And if not ..., unclean, because ...

    5. 2:6A-C: A spoiled jar ... before ... clean, after ..., unclean.
*   6. 2:6D-F: A sprinkler is clean (Eleazer). A sprinkler is unclean (Yosé), because ...
The dispute, when restated as declarative sentences, preserves the contrast of its setting.
    7. 2:7I: That which serves ... unclean, and that which serves clean.
[* 8. 2:8C-D: The comb is clean ... is unclean (dispute-components).]
[* 9. 3:5: See List 4, No. 1.]
[10. 3:7A-B: See List 4, No. 3.]
[11. 3:7F: See List 1, No. 3. Copper vessels lines ... clean, but if ... unclean.]
[12. 3:8A-B: See List 4, No. 4.]
[* 13. 3:8D-H: See List 1, No. 4.]
[* 14. 4:1A-D: See List 1, No. 5.]
    15. 4:3D, E-F: Any part which ... receives uncleanness by contact, airspace, any
part which + not ..., contact, not airspace. E-F likewise present the same contrast.
[* 16. 4:4A-D: See List 4, No. 6.]
[* 17. 5:3B, D-E: See List 1, No. 8.]
[18. 5:5: See List 1, No. 10.]
    19. 5:6: See List 1, No. 11, contact <u>vs.</u> airspace.
[20. 5:7, F: Unclean, clean. See List 1, No. 12.]
[* 21. 5:10A-C: Unclean, clean. See List 1, No. 15.]
[22. 5:10D-E: Unclean, clean. See List 2, No. 11.]
[* 23. 5:11A, E-F, G-H, I: clean, unclean. See List 1, No. 16.]
[24. 6:1A-B <u>vs.</u> C-D, E <u>vs.</u> G-H: Unclean, clean. See List 4, No. 7.]
[25. 6:3D, E, J-L: See List 5, No. 2.]
[26. 6:4: See List 5, No. 2.]
[27. 7:2: See List 1, No. 18.]
[28. 7:3: See List 1, No. 19.]
[29. 7:4: See List 1, No. 20.]
[30. 7:5-6: See List 1, Nos. 21-22.]
[* 31. 8:1G-I: Unclean, clean.]
[32. 8:4A-C <u>vs.</u> D-E: Unclean, clean. See List 5, No. 7.]
[33. 8:6A-C: See List 5, No. 9.]
[34. 10:7A-C: See List 5, No. 12.]
35. 11:4A-D, F-G (+ H-K): Unclean iron smelted with clean, if ... unclean, unclean,
and if ... clean, clean. Half and half -- unclean.
*   36. 11:5A (+ B-D): Scorpion-bit ... is unclean. And that of cheeks is clean.
*   37. 11:6 + B (C), D, E-F (+ G-I): As above.
    38. 11:7A + B (+ C-F), H: As above.
    39. 12:1A-B, C-D, E + F-G, H + I: Unclean, clean.
    40. 12:2C: Clean, unclean.
    41. 12:2D, E, F (+ G This is the general rule): unclean, clean.
*   42. 12:3 (A-C + D) E, F, G: Unclean, clean.
*   43. 12:4A: Unclean, clean Sadoq.

44. 12:5A-B + disputes: Unclean, clean.

45. 13:4C, D-E: Clean, unclean; unclean, clean.

46. 13:5A, B, D, E: Clean, unclean -- 4X

47. 13:A + B-C, D (+ E): Unclean, clean. A: Wood subsidiary to metal, unclean, metal/wood -- clean, etc.

48. 13:8A, B-C (+ D-E): Unclean, clean.

[49. 14:3C: See List 1, No. 38.]

*   50. 14:6: A basket cover etc. (Judah declares clean, sages) unclean. Metal mirror is clean. Sages' position yields contrastive predicate.

*   51. 15:2A + B (C-D), F, G-H (+ I-J): Baking boards of ... are unclean and of ... clean, etc. A parallels F, G/H.

52. 15:3A (+ B-C): As above.

[53. 15:4A, B: See List 1, No. 42.]

[54. 15:5A, B: See List 1, No. 43.]

*   55. 15:6A, B, C-D, F: Unclean, clean.

56. 16:5A, B, C-D: Unclean, clean, clean, unclean, unclean, clean (= - +, + -, - +).

57. 16:6A-B (+ C) + D: This is general rule: unclean, clean.

*   58. 17:3B-C + D: A basket which ... is unclean. [If] one made ..., it is clean.

#* 59. 17:17A, B, C (+ D-F, G, H, I): Base of ... is unclean ... and of ... is clean, etc.

[60. 18:3G-H: Unclean ... clean. See List 1, NO. 52.]

[61. 18:5A-C: See List 1, No. 54.]

*   62. 26:2A-B, C-H): A laced up bag ... is unclean. [If] it is made flat, it is clean.

63. 26:3A-B, C-D: Clean, unclean, unclean, clean (= + -, - +).

[64. 27:3: See List 4, No. 30.]

[65. 28:9F-G: See List 4, No. 33.]

66. 30:1D-E, F-G: Clean, unclean (2X)

[67. 30:2: See List 1, No. 90.]

[68. 30:3E: Unclean, clean.]

69. 30:4A-D: Unclean, clean, clean, unclean.

Ohalot

[70. 5:4B, E: See List 4, No. 36.]

[71. 6:2A, B, D: See List 5, No. 22.]

[72. 6:3C: See List 5, No. 23.]

[73. 6:4A, C, D, E: See List 5, No. 24.]

[74. 9:1-14: See List 5, No. 31.]

[75. 15:10A-B: See List 4, No. 54.]

Hereinafter, only significant exempla are listed.

Negaim

76. 11:2A-D: Camel's hair and sheep's wool ... if longer ..., not susceptible ... susceptible ...

Parah: --

Tohorot: --

Miqvaot: --

Niddah: --

Makhshirin: --
    [77. 2:2C-E, 2:3-11: See above, No. 35.]

Zabim: --

Tebul Yom: --

Yadayim: --

Uqsin: --

4. **He Who ... it is ... -- Apocopation**
    In these sentences, the formulary distinction is in the subject of the sentences. Here we will have a construction in which the predicate carries forward not the subject of one who, but the complement or object of the sentence beginning one who, or to an implied object thereof. This is referred to in the analytical volumes as mild apocopation. A good example of this sort of disjuncture between subject and predicate is:
    He who cooks a chicken for three hours -- it [the chicken, not the cook] is
    edible.
The difference between mild and extreme apocopation is not always sure. One may well make a case for moving items on the present list to that which follows, though, in my judgment, none on List 5 can be properly located here. In italics is the subject of the predicate, clearly apocopated, and different, from the subject of the sentence's subject-clause.

Kelim
*   1. 3:5: He who plasters ..., Meir + Simeon declare [the lining formed by the plaster] unclean. And sages say, He who plasters ... the [layer] is clean, and [the layer] is unclean.
    2. 3:6A: The scutchgrass with which they line ..., that which touches it [= scutchgrass] is unclean. B + C are simple declarative sentences, appended to A.
    3. 3:7A-B: [As to] a kettle which one lined with mortar and clay, that which touches the mortar is unclean, that which touches clay is clean.
    4. 3:8A-B: A jar which ... and repaired with pitch more than needed, that which touches needed pitch is unclean, excess, clean.

5. 3:8C-D: Pitch which dripped ... that which touches it is clean.

*   6. 4:4A-D: A clay vessel which has three rims [If] the innermost ... all are clean. [If] ... all are unclean. [if] ..., unclean, clean. [If] all equal, (Judah says) they divide the middle one, etc.

7. 6:1A-B, C-D, E, G-H: He who makes ... and joined them ..., it [what is thereby made] is unclean. [If] he fixed ..., it [the tripod] is clean, etc.

8. 8:5A-B (+ C-D), E-G + H: A cock which swallowed ... and fell ... of the oven, it [the oven] is clean. E-G: The insect which is found in the oven, the bread which is in it [the oven] is unclean. This second sentence is more severely apocopated than the first.

*   9. 8:10A-C, D-E, F-G or H (+ I, J-K): One unclean ... who had food and liquids ..., [if] he poked ..., they [= liquids] have made it unclean.

10. 8:11A-B + C (+ D-E): The unclean woman from whose breasts ... into the airspace of the oven, it [oven] is unclean.

*   11. 9:2A-D: A jar which is filled ... and a siphon is in it ... House of Shammai: Jar and liquids are clean, siphon is unclean, etc.

12. 9:3A-C + D, D-E + F, G-I: The insect which is found below ... oven, it [the oven] is clean, etc.

13. 9:4A-B + C (D-E): A sponge which absorbed ..., it [oven] is unclean ...

14. 9:5A-C + D (+ E-H): Sherds which ... and fell into ... oven, [if] the oven was heated, it [= the oven] is unclean.

15. 9:6A-C: Olive-peat etc. ... and unclean ... walked on them, and liquids exuded, they [liquids] are clean.

16. 10:6A-C (+ D-F): A jar which was perforated and which the wine-lees have stopped up -- the [= wine-lees] have afforded protection for it.

*   17. 11:8D-E, F-G (+ H, I): A necklace whose beads are on a thread ... if the thread is broken, the beads are unclean, because ...

18. 11:9: As above.

19. 17:13C: He who makes ... it is unclean.

20. 17:15A, B, C, D-E: He who makes ... it is unclean (4X).

21. 19:1A: He who unties the bed ... he who touches the ropes is clean. This may be deemed extreme apocopation.

22. 19:2A-B (+ C-D): The rope which hangs over ... up to five handbreadths [of the rope] is clean, etc.

*   23. 19:3A, C, D-E: The bedgirth which hangs over ... any amount [thereof is unclean], so Meir.

24. 10:5A (+ declarative sentences, if understood, at B, C, D, E, F): A bed which was unclean, and around which one wrapped ..., the whole is unclean.

25. 19:6A-B (+ C, D, E, F-G, H-I): As above.

26. 19:8B-C: The goatskin, the bags of which contain, and [the bags] were damaged, [the bags] are clean, because ...

27. 20:7F + G: He who loosens ..., it is unclean.

28. 25:6A-B, C, D (E-F): Bases of utensils on which ..., one dries them, etc.

(29. 26:9A + B, C, D: A hide which ... Once one has ..., it is clean, so Judah.)

30. 27:3A-C, D-E + F: He who makes ..., it is clean.

*   31. 27:4A-B, C-D, E-G: He who cuts ..., it is unclean.

*   32. 28:3A (+ B-D): He who makes ... it is clean.

33. 28:9F-G + H: He who makes ... it is clean.

Ohalot

34. 3:2A-B (+C) D (+ E-G): A ladleful of corpse-mould which was scattered -- the house is unclean.

*#   35. 5:1A-D: An oven which is standing ..., and the cortege overshadowed ... (House of Shammai say) the whole is unclean.

(#   36. 5:2A-D + 5:3, 5:4A-B + C, D-E + F-G: A flagon which is ..., the flagon is ..., and the liquids are ...)

*#   37. 9:15A, B, C, D: A tomb which is ... and the corpse is ... -- he who touches, etc.

38. 13:1A: He who makes ..., its measure is -- see List 2, No. 26.

*   39. 15:8A-B, C (+ D-E): The forecourt of the tomb-vault -- he who stands ... is clean, etc.

40. 15:9A, B: [A jar which], he who touches it is ...

41. 15:10A, B, (+ C): He who touches ..., they are unclean, etc.

42. 17:4: A field which is ..., if rains ..., they do not make ...

43. 18:2: As above.

Negaim

44. 11:1C-D: [He who buys], let them be examined afresh.

45. 11:4A-C: Garment, warp of which is ... -- everything follows the status of what is apparent.

#*   46. 11:5A, B, C, D-F, G-H, I-J: [That which stands], let it [= garment] be washed, etc.

*   47. 11:9A-G *+ H-J): [He who winds from one coil to another ... on one of which ..., lo, the] second is clean.

48. 11:10F-H: A shirt on which a plague appeared -- it [the plague] affords ...

(49. 11:11F-G (+ H-I): A blanket on which (Eliezer b. Jacob says) [it does not ...] until ...)

50. 11:12A-B (+ C), D-E (+F): A garment which has been shut up which was mixed among -- they all are ... (2X).

51. 12:1B: He who buys -- they are ...

52. 13:1: Ten [conditions]: That which ... and that which -- one scrapes it and it is clean, so B-C, D-E, F-G. The remainder are [if]-clauses.

Parah

53. 2:2A: A cow whose ..., let one chop [them] off.

*   54. 2:5G-J: There were on it ... -- all follows ...

55. 5:8A-C (+ D-G): Two troughs which are ..., one mixed (in) one of them -- water in the second is ...

56. 5:9A-D (+ E-F): Two stones which ... -- <u>water</u> between them is ...

57. 6:1A-E (+ F-I): He who mixes ... and the ash fell ..., <u>it</u> is unfit.

58. 6:3A-C (+ D-G): He who mixes ... the <u>water</u> which is in it ...

59. 6:5A-B: He who diverts ..., <u>it</u> is ...

60. 7:1A-C, D-E, F-G (+ H-I): Five who drew -- low, <u>all</u> is ...

61. 7:2A-D + G, 7:3A-C, D-E, F: As above.

62. 7:4A (B, C, D): [<u>He who says</u> -- demanded in the context on M. 7:1FF.] ..., <u>the first</u> is ...

63. 7:6A-B + C, D: He who brings ..., <u>it</u> is suitable.

64. 7:7A (+ B, C): He who wraps ... -- <u>it</u> [water] is fit.

#*   65. 7:8A-C (+ D), E (+ G-H); 7:9A-F (+ G-I); 7:10A (+ B-C); 7:11A-C + D (+ E); 7:12A (+B), C (+ B-E); 8:1A-C (+ D-E, F-L): He who ..., <u>it</u> [water, not mentioned in the protasis. is ...

66. 9:1A-C + D-E (F-I): A flask into which ... (Eliezer says), One sprinkles ... Dew fell ... (Eliezer says), Let <u>him</u> leave it ...

67. 9:5A-B (+C-H): Water which has been made ... -- one should not trample <u>it</u> ...

*   68. 9:6A-B (+ E-F); 9:7A (+ B-D): As above.

69. 11:1A-B (+ C-I): A jar which one left ..., it [<u>the water</u>] is unfit.

70. 11:3A-D: A ring which fell into water and which one removed ..., <u>the water</u> is ... (+ E-J).

71. 12:6A-E: He who sprinkles with ..., <u>the water</u> is ...

Tohorot

72. 5:7A-D (+E-K): He who sat down ... because of ..., they burn, and as to ..., <u>they follow</u> ...

73. 5:8E-I: He on whose garments ... if ..., his <u>garments</u> are ...

74. 7:1A-C (+D), E-F; 7:2, 7:3, 7:4, 7:5, 7:6, 7:7, 7:8, 7:9, 8:1, 8:2, 8:3, 8:4, 8:5: Long sequence of <u>he-who</u> ... <u>it is</u> ... -- constructions

*   75. 9:5A-C (+D-H): He who leaves ..., lo, <u>these</u> are ...

76. 9:6A-C (+ D-I): As above.

77. 10:2A-D, E-F + G-J: Olive-worders who were ..., and unclean liquids were ..., if there is ..., lo, <u>these</u> are clean.

Miqvaot

*   78. 2:6: He who scrapes up ... <u>it</u> is fit.

79. 2:10A + B (C-M): A pool which contains ... water and mud -- <u>they</u> dunk in ...

#*   80. 3:3E-M, 3:4C-F: Two who were pouring ..., this one pours ..., this one pours ..., he who wrings], and he who empties ..., (^CAqiva declares) [<u>the pool</u>] is fit ..., etc.

*   81. 5:5D-G, H: Dripping water which one made ..., <u>one</u> sticks in ...

82. 5:6A-C: A wave which broke off and fell on man and utensils -- <u>they</u> are clean.

Niddah

*   83. 4:6A-C (+ D-H): She who is ... any <u>blood</u> which she sees is clean until ...

84. 10:5A (+ B, C, D): The woman who died and from whom a drop of blood exuded -- it imparts ...

* 85. 10:8A-B + C (+D-J): She who sees blood and immersed and had intercourse -- (House of Shammai say) they impart uncleanness ...

Makhshirin

86. 2:2C-E + 2:3A-D (+ 2:4-11, above: The pool which is in the house, the house sweats on its account, if it was unclean, and the sweat is unclean, etc.

#* 87. 3:1A-E: A sack full of pieces of fruit which one placed ... and they absorbed ..., all [the pieces of fruit] under ... + 3:2A-D (+ E-H), 3:3A + B, C, D-E; 3:4A-D, E-G, H (+ I-J): 3:5A-C, D, E-F, G-L.

88. 3:8A-B, C-E (+ F, G, H-I): He who brings down ..., lo, this is under the law ...

#* 89. 4:1A-B (+C), D-E (+ F-H), 4:2A-C (+ D-H), 4:3A (+B): He who kneels ... the water which ... is ...

#* 90. 4:5F-G: A trough into which ..., the drops that splashed are not ... (+ H-J), K-N (=O), P-Q + R (+S).

91. 4:6A-B (+C-E), F-G *+ H), 4:7A-C (+D): A basket which is ..., one puts out his hand ...

* 92. 7:9A-B + C: He who draws ... up to three days, it ...

#* 93. 5:1A-B (+C-F), 5:2A-C (+ D-E), F-G, 5:3, 5:4A-C + D: He who immersed ..., the second renders ..., 5:2A-C: he who swam ... the water which splashed is not ...

94. 5:6A-C (+D-F): He who beat ... [what is splashed] is ...

95. 5:7D, E, F + G: He who takes (3X) -- lo, this is under ...

96. 5:8A-C + D: A covering ... [rain which falls thereon] is not ...

#* 97. 5:10A-D, E-F, G-I, 5:11A-D (+ E-H, I), J-K + L-M, 6:1A-C (+ D-G), 6:2A-C: He who empties ... it [the remaining water] is ..., etc.

Zabim

98. 4:1A-B (+ C, D): A menstruating woman who sat with ... -- the cap which is on her head [= the other woman's head] is ...

*# 99. 4:1E: A Zab who knocked against the balcony and a loaf fell -- it [the loaf] is ... + 4:2A-C.

* 100. 4:4A-C (+ D-I): A Zab who was lying ..., lengthwise -- they are unclean, etc.

Tebun Yom

#* 101. 1:1A-B + C: He who collects ... (House of Shammai say), It is deemed connected ... 10:1D-E, F-J + K-M; 1:2 (as in the foregoing).

*# 102. 2:3A-B, C-D (+ E-H), 2:4A-B + C, 2:5A-B (+ C-G), H-I + J: The porridge ... and the garlic, part of which a Tebul Yom touched ... he has rendered this whole unfit, etc.

103. 2:7E-F: He who pours ... and a Tebul Yom touched ..., it is neutralized ...

104. 3:2A-C (+ D-E): A vegetable which is ..., and a beaten egg is placed ..., and a Tebul Yom touched the egg -- he has rendered unfit only the stalk [not mentioned in the protasis]...

#*   105. 3:4E-G, 3:5A-C, 3:6A-C, D-G (H-K, L-N): Dough which was ... and which a
Tebul Yom touched (Eleazar b. Judah says) -- he has rendered the entire mixture unfit.

[106. 4:1: See List 5, No. 101.]

107. 4:4A-C: A flagon which is ..., if he said ..., lo, this is heave-offering ... (+ E-F).

*   108. 4:7A-B: He who gave ... and said ... -- [his statement means]...

Yadayim

*   109. 3:1A-B or C (+ D-L): He who pokes his hands into ... -- his hands are ...

Uqsin

110. 2:5A (+ B-C): He who chops -- it is not ... [See List 1. No. 272.]

5. Extreme Apocopation

Here the several stichs of the subject of a sentence not only do not relate to the
implied or stated subject of the predicate, exhibiting complete disjuncture therefrom, but
also may not relate to one another. What gives the sentence order and meaning is the
context established by the individual units or clauses; there is no mistaking the meaning.

Kelim

1. 6:2A-D, E-F: A stone on which ..., on it and on, [on it and on], it is unclean, etc.

2. 6:3A-D (+E), F-H (+ I-M): Three stones of which one made ..., one of the outer
ones became unclean, the middle -- that which serves is unclean ... clean. Both were
made unclean, if the middle stone was large, one gives to this [outer stone] sufficient
space ..., and the next is clean, etc.

3. 6:4: Two stones which one ..., and which were made unclean, [if] one ..., half of
this one is unclean, and half ... clean. The predicate does not refer to the subject of the
opening clause, but to its own, dependent predicate.

4. 8:1A-C, D-F (+G-I + J-K: full sentences): The oven which one divided with
hangings, an insect is found in any place, the whole is unclean, etc.

5. 8:2A-C (+ D-E), F-H, I-J (+ K-L): As above.

6. 8:3A-C (+ D-E), F-H, I-K: As above.

7. 8:4A-C (+ D-E): As above. Note that after the apocopated inaugural clauses, we
regularly find simple declarative sentences.

8. 8:5E-G: See List 4, No. 8.

9. 8:6A-C (+ D-E): A leaven-pot with a tight cover in an oven, the leaven and
insect are in it and the partition is between them -- the oven is unclean, and the leaven
clean.

10. 8:7A-B (+ C, D-E + F): The insect which is found ... from the inner rim ... it
[the oven] is clean ... See List 1, No. 23.

11. 9:1A-D (+ E, F-H, I-J, K, L, M-O): A needle ... found in the ground, seen but not
project ... if one bakes dough and it touches them [needle, etc.] it [= oven] is unclean.

12. 10:7A-C + D, E-F: An old oven inside a new, and a colander is over the mouth
..., [if] one removed ... and the colander falls, the whole is unclean. And if not, clean.

This seems to me apocopated, in that the whole does not refer back to any one clause of the protasis, but to the unstated result of the whole.

13. 10:8A-E (F, I-J, K-L, M-N): As above, and clearly apocopated.

14. 18:8A-B: A head phylactery -- one untied the first and repaired it, etc. -- it [the repaired part] is unclean ... The remainder continues in simple declarative sentences.

Ohalot

15. 3:4B, C, D-E: (The corpse is outside and hair inside -- the house is unclean, etc.) Two bones, and on them are two ..., one brought part of them inside, and the house overshadows them -- it is unclean.

16. 3:5G: A crucified man whose blood gushes forth, and under whom is found a quarter-log -- it [= blood] is unclean.

17. 3:7A (Generalization) + C-F, G-I, J-L, M-P, Q-S, T-U. (+ V-Y): A drain which is ... uncleanness is in it -- the house is ... uncleanness is in the house -- what is in it is clean, for ... It is ... uncleanness is in it -- the house is unclean, etc.

*# 18. 4:1A-C, D-E + F, G-I, J-L, M-P; 4:2A-D, E-G + H; 4:3A-C, D-F, G-I (+ J-L): As above (10X).

19. 5:6B-C (+ D, E, F, G-H): Cistern and cellar which are in the house and a basket is placed on it -- it is clean.

20. 5:7A (Generalization) +B, C-E + F, G-I + J-K: A basket which is ..., uncleanness is under it -- utensils which are in the basket are clean.

*# 21. 6:1A (Generalization) + B, C + D, E, F: As above.

22. 6:2A + B, C: [Corpse-bearers who were], and one of them shut the door and fastened it with the key -- if the door can stand by itself, it is unclean, etc.

* 23. 6:3A (Generalization) + B, C, D-E. As above.

24. 6:4A, B, C, D, E (+ F): As above.

25. 6:6A (Generalization) + B + C, D, E: As above.

26. 6:7C, D + E-F: Uncleanness and utensils which are ..., if there is ..., they [= utensils] are unclean, etc.

27. 7:1C, D + E-F: A second wall -- uncleanness breaks forth and ascends, etc.

#* 28. 7:2A (Generalization) B, C, D, E, F, G, H: A tent which slopes ... uncleanness is in the tent -- utensils which are under the wall are unclean, etc.

29. 7:4A (+ B, C, + 7:5): The woman who was ... and they removed her, the first [house] is unclean, etc.

30. 7:6A (+B): The woman who is in hard labor -- they chop up, etc.

31. 9:1-15: A hive which is ..., about an olive's bulk ... is placed ..., whatever is ... is unclean. And whatever is ... is clean.

32. 9:16A, B, C + D-E, F: A jar which is ..., and corpse-matter is placed], uncleanness breaks forth ..., and the jar is unclean, etc.

*# 33. 10:1-7: A hatchway which is ..., and there is ..., uncleanness is in the house -- that which ... Uncleanness is ... -- the house is clean, etc.

*# 34. 11:1-2: The house which split -- uncleanness is -- utensils which are ... are clean, etc.

*   35. 11:8: The cellar which is in the house, and a candlestick is in it, and its cup
projected, and a basket was set, etc. + Houses: The cellar is clean, and the candlestick is
unclean, etc.

       37. 12:2: As above.

       38. 12:3A (+ B, C): As above.

       39. 12:4A + B: As above

       40. 12:5A, B, C, D: As above

       41. 12:6A (+B): As above

       42. 12:7: As above

43. 14:4A, B: A projection which runs ..., uncleanness is ..., utensils which are
underneath ... are unclean.

44. 14:5A-D, E + F-G: As above.

46. 14:6: As above.

47. 14:7: As above.

48. 15:2A (+ B, C): Tables of wood which touch ..., uncleanness is ..., he who
touches the second is unclean, etc.

49. 15:3A (+B), C-D: As above.

50. 15:4A, B, C: As above.

51. 15:5A, B-C, +D: As above.

52. 15:6A, B + C: As above.

       53. 15:7: As above.

       54. 15:10D: Two houses, and in them are ..., he put his two hands, if there is in his
hands, he brings ...

       55. 16:1A (Generalization) (+ B-C) - 16:2A + B, (C), D + E: A spindle which is
thrust, corpse-matter is ..., even though they ... -- it is unclean.

Negaim

       56. 4:4-11: Bright spot-sequence.

57. 5:1A-B (Generalization) C-H: He on whom was ..., at the end of one week, and
behold ..., doubt that ..., doubt that ..., he is unclean.

58. 5:2A-F, G-L, M-R: As above.

       59. 5:3 A-C (Generalization) + E-F, K-M: As above.

*   60. 5:4A-B (Generalization) + E-J: Two who came ... on this is ... and on this is ...
at the end of a week ... and it is not known ..., etc.

       61. 5:5A (Generalization) + C-F (+ G-I): As above.

*#   62. 6:1 (Generalization), 6:2A-F, 6:3A-C, D, E-I; 6:4A-C: As above.

*   63. 6:5A-D (+ E-H), 6:6 J-K, L-M: As above.

       64. 7:3A-B, C, D-F, G-I, J-L: A bright spot -- in it there is nothing -- in the first
instance, etc.

*#   65. 8:2A-G, H-L, 8:3A-E, F-I: A bright spot, and in it is ..., it broke forth ..., he is
...

       66. 8:5A, B (Generalization) + C + D-G, H-M: [If] it ..., [if then] ..., the boil and
burning ..., they are ...

67. 8:6A-E (+ F-P): Two bright spots, one unclean, one clean, it broke forth ..., and afterward ..., he is clean.

68. 8:7A: He who ... let him be shut up. C-E (+ F-I): [If] two of them ..., etc., the boil and quick flesh, etc. ..., quick flesh appeared ..., he is unclean.

[69. 8:10G-J: See List 1, No. 123.]

\# 70. 10:5A-C (Generalization) D-I, J-O: One certified ..., the golden hair went away, ... returned, in the first ..., lo, this one is as it/he was, etc.

\# 71. 10:6A-D, E-F (G-H), I-J; 10:7A-D, E-F (G-H), I-J: As above.

* 72. 11:6E-G (+ H-J): He who attaches ..., a plague recurred ..., he burns the patch.

* 73. 11:6E-G (+ H-J): A summer garment which has ... checks -- they [= plagues] spread ...

* 74. 13:3A-C (+ D-E, F-G, H-K): A house on which ..., there was ... on top of it ..., one assigns the beams to ...

* 75. 13:11A-C (+ D-F+ 13:12A-C): A leper who entered the house - all the utensils ... are unclean.

Parah

76. 12:2A-C, D-E, F-H (+ I-T): One sprinkled -- it is in doubt whether ... -- his sprinkling is valid, etc.

77. 12:4A (+ B-F): He who sprinkles ... [the one who got wet] entered ... he [the one who got wet] is ...

\# 78. 12:6F (Generalization), 12:7, 12:8A-B (+ C-D = 12:6F): He who is clean ... whose hands became unclean -- his body is ... (3X).

Tohorot

79. 2:1A-C (+ D-N): Woman who was ... and touched a loaf ... even though it is ... it is ...

\# 80. 4:1A-D (+ G-F), 4:2A-D, 4:3A-F (+ G-K): He who threw ..., it is ... creeping thing is ..., and it walks ..., doubt whether or not ..., its doubt is ...

81. 4:4A-D, E-F, G-H: As above.

82. 4:6A-G (+ H-K): Two ..., one ... and one ..., they suspend ...

83. 5:1: The several clauses are totally apocopated.

\#* 84. 5:3A-E (+F-J), 5:4A-D (+E-G), 5:5A-C + D-E + F, 5:5A-C + D-E + F: Two paths, one unclean, one clean, one walked in one of them ..., lo, these are clean, etc.

*\# 85. 6:2 (A + B) C-F, G, H, I + J-K: As above. 6:3A-D, E-G, H-J, etc.; 6:4A-C (Generalization), E-F, G-H, I-J, K-L, M-N, O-Q + R-S.

86. 8:8A-C (+ D-I): Kneading trough which lay ..., and the dough is ..., and running liquid is ..., three pieces ..., they are not ...

87. 9:8A-B (+ C-I): The dead creeping thing which is ..., unclean is only the place which ...

* 88. 10:1A-B + D-F: He who locks ..., utensils were there ..., the olive press is ...

89. 10:5A-C (+ D-N): He who eats ..., even though they burst ..., lo, the press is ...

90. 10:6: He who was ..., it is doubt ..., the doubt is ...

91. 10:7A-B (+ C-Q): He who emptied, and a dead creeping thing was found -- all are ...

Miqvaot

*# 92. 2:1, 2:2A-E, I-O, 2:3A-F + G: Unclean person who went down to immerse, it is a doubt whether ..., and even if ..., it is a doubt whether ..., two immersion pools ..., he immersed in one of them. etc. -- his doubt is deemed unclean.

93. 4:1A-D (+ E-J): He who leaves utensils ..., it [the water] spoils the pool.

94. 4:2A-D + E: He who leaves ..., it spoils ... [it = water gathered in the tray] ...

95. 4:3A-C (+ D-K): He who makes a cavity ..., [if it is] of wood [it spoils pool at] any amount at all, etc.

96. 4:4A-E (+ F-K): Drawn water and fit water which mingled ..., if greater part is from fit, it [= immersion-pool] is fit, etc.

97. 6:3A-I (+ J-N): Three pools ..., in this one are ..., and three people went down ..., and it was mingled ..., the pools are clean ..., and the people are clean ...

98. 6:11A-D (+ E-J): Filter of batch ... lower pipe is ... and upper is ..., if in front ..., if [= the pool, not mentioned heretofore] is unfit.

* 99. 7:6A-C (+ D-F), G-I (+ J-K), 7:7 (A-D), E-J (K-N): A pool which contains ..., two people went down ..., the first is clean, the second unclean. The cushion or mattress of leather, once one has lifted ..., the water in them is deemed ... A pool, the water of which is ..., one presses down ... and goes down and immerses.

Niddah: None.

Makhshirin

100. 1:1-6: See above.

Zabim: None.

Tebul Yom

[101. 3:2A-C: See List 4, No. 104.]

102. 4:1A-C + D: Produce of tithe which was ..., and which ... or ... -- they separate from it ...

Yadayim

103. 2:4A-D, E (Generalization) +F, G, then H-K, L-N, O-Q, R-T, V: extreme and extended, balanced apocopation.

Uqsin: None.

Let us now compare the distribution, among the several tractates of our order, of simple declarative sentences, exempla in which mild apocopation governs the formulation of the whole, and those characterized by extreme apocopation.

Tractate	Number of Chapters	Proportion of Whole	Simple Declarative Sentences	Proportion of Whole	Mild Apocopation	Proportion of Whole	Extreme Apocopation	Proportion of Whole
Kelim	30	23.8%	92	33.3%	32	29.0%	14	13.4%
Ohalot	18	14.2%	21	7.6%	10	9.0%	41	39.4%
Negaim	14	11.1%	36	13.0%	10	9.0%	21	20.1%
Parah	12	9.5%	25	9.0%	19	17.2%	3	2.8%
Tohorot	10	7.9%	21	7.6%	6	5.4%	13	12.5%
Miqvaot	10	7.9%	19	6.8%	5	4.5%	8	7.6%
Niddah	10	7.9%	24	8.6%	3	2.7%	---	---
Makhshirin	6	4.7%	10	3.6%	12	10.9%	1	0.9%
Zabim	5	3.9%	8	2.8%	3	2.7%	---	---
Tebul Yom	4	3.1%	9	3.2%	8	7.2%	2	1.9%
Yadayim	4	3.1%	2	0.7%	1	0.9%	1	0.9%
Uqsin	3	2.3%	9	3.2%	1	0.9%	---	---
	126	99.4%	276	99.4%	110	99.4%	104	99.5%

Among the patterns under discussion, we observe disproportions which indicate a preference of a given formulary pattern for a given topic, in the case of apocopation in Kelim, Ohalot, Negaim, Parah, Tohorot, and Makhshirin. These tractates among themselves, however, are sufficiently diverse so that we cannot claim that there was a sense of "appropriate" correspondence between apocopation and some one topic of law. Apocopation rather seems to serve to give formal structure to cases or exemplifications of generalizations, e.g., matters of doubt for Tohorot. There do appear to be too many declarative sentences in Kelim, and the disproportion would appear more striking if we treated lists as extended, but syntactically tight and smooth declarative sentences. Otherwise the distribution seems to be even.

    With the evident disproportions taken into account, we gain the impression that the use of the several patterns is random for the one pattern which is least distinctive, the declarative sentence, just as is the case with the dispute. I may therefore maintain that the document as a whole has been subjected to a fairly consistent scheme of formalized formulation. But that is the case only if I can show that even the declarative sentence, surely "merely the way people say things," in fact exhibits traits of formalization and discipline. For this purpose I must return the consideration of the intermediate divisions in behalf of which I have alleged that the simple declarative sentence constitutes evidence of externally-unitary formulary cogency.

iii. Tradents and Redactors or Tradent-Redactors? The Mnemonic Factor
    Our first examination of the way in which cognitive units are strung together into intermediate divisions ("chapters") shows that coherent formulary patterns characterize sizable sequences of cognitive units on a single theme. These traits, common to a series

of distinct cognitive units, are redactional, because they are imposed at that point at which someone intended to join together discrete (finished) units on a given theme. The varieties of traits particular to the discrete units and the diversity of authorities cited therein, including masters of two or three or even four strata from the turn of the first century to the end of the second, make it highly improbable that the several units were formulated in a common pattern and then preserved, until, later on, still further units, on the same theme and in the same pattern, were worked out and added. The entire indifference, moreover, to historical order of authorities and concentration on the logical unfolding of a given theme or problem without reference to the sequence of authorities, confirm the supposition that the work of formulation and that of redaction go forward together.

When we have sizable constructions of cognitive units (Chapter Two, section ii), all of them conforming to a single, highly distinctive formulary pattern, which itself is internal to the expression of the ideas stated therein, we have no reason whatsoever to doubt that the whole was both made up and put together by one and the same hand. In such constructions the tradental and redactional work is coincident. The other, and principal, sort of intermediate division (Chapter Two, Section iii), that in which an externally-unitary formulary pattern is applied to a single theme or problem, has now to be reconsidered. Having a clear notion of the gross formulary pattern which characterize all of those many intermediate divisions distinguished by a common theme and a common formulary pattern consisting of "simple declarative sentences," we now refine our earlier results. Our interest is in the intermediate divisions whose externally-unitary formulary trait has been designated as the presence of the "simple declarative sentence." Accordingly, we review Chapter Two, Section iii, with reference to the specified entries.

Kelim

iii. 2: Duplicated subject, "The measure ... that which is made ..."

iii. 3: This subdivision is to be further segmented, since 3:3-4 form extended declarative sentences with no apocopation, while 3:6-8 shifts to the duplicated subject. The theme, moreover, is hardly identical. 3:5 should then be understood to introduce 3:6-8, for its theme is congruent to what follows, that is, the status of materials with which one lines a clay utensil. (Once more, the he-who formulary serves to introduce a new unit of material, though I am not sure that that function is normative.) The whole structure most certainly does focus upon a single theme, although I think it is clear that it is made up of two prior components.

iii. 4: The formulary pattern resumes that of 3:3-4. But has the subject changed? If we look back at 3:3-4, we see that the point of the unit is to specify when a utensil ceases to be subject to uncleanness, which is when the status of utensil falls away from it. In point of fact 4:1-4 make exactly that point with reference to specific items, and perhaps we should therefore regard the whole as interrupted by iii. 3.

iii. 5: Duplicated subject.

iii. 6: These are simple declarative sentences, fairly richly augmented by subordinate clauses, An oven which ..., or which ... or which ..., is unclean. There certainly is a clear shift in formulary pattern from the foregoing, and a consistent mode of expression in the listed sentences.

iii. 8: Once more, simple declarative sentences are used in a long sequence, and each entry tends to bear its share of subordinate clauses, The firebasket of ..., which was ..., is unclean, for one ..., so 7:1. The hob of a stove which has ..., is clean as ..., and unclean as ... There clearly is some subordinate formalization, x unclean/y clean, e.g., at 7:2, 3, 4. 7:2 also exhibits a duplicated subject, Its sides -- that which touches them ... What is decisive is that at the outset of each cognitive unit we find the expected formulary pattern.

iii. 12: Here is a fine example of the diversity of the simple declarative sentence. There is no difficulty in distinguishing this subdivision, e.g., from 3:3-4/6-8, even though both fall within the category of simple declarative sentence. Moreover, we notice that the pattern before us is without parallel in our entire tractate.

iii. 13: Once more, the simple declarative sentence exhibits its capacity for distinctiveness and diversity. The sentences are fully worked out, with subordinate clauses, and are readily discerned from the sort at iii. 12 and iii. 14.

iii. 14: Here, as noted, we do not find equivalently tightly formulary sentences. Yet the x unclean/y clean-pattern does impose a shift in the diction of the sentences, from fully worked out and smooth ones, to contrastive constructions. What is important is that the contrast -- x this/y that -- is effected even where the apodosis is undifferentiated, that is, at 13:7, and the point of emphasis is the lo, these are.

iii. 15: While it is true that the common form is the dispute, the components of the dispute are strikingly balanced with one another through 15:1F-S. 15:2's sentences are built on the contrastive apodosis, and the dispute is incidental to the sentence-structure. The same applies to 15:3. The point made above, that the contrastive apodosis is present even without the x unclean/y clean-formulation, is to be applied at 15:4. This brings us back to 15:1F-S, for there is no better example of the contrastive apodosis than that which is present in the two long and complex, highly-tuned balanced clauses, of Meir's and Judah's sayings. Accordingly, the contrastive predicate, not merely the dispute, is what constitutes the formulary unity of the entire construction, an impressive one at that.

iii. 16: A second look shows us that this set is built out of the contrastive predicate, and one can make a case in favor of regarding iii. 15 and 16 as a single formulary subdivision.

iii. 17: Duplicated subject.

iii. 18: The continuation of the duplicated subject and of the theme of the point at which various objects and materials receive uncleanness suggest that iii. 17 and 18 may be deemed a single intermediate division. The unclean/clean-pattern then is secondary to the redactional intent.

iii. 19: There can be no clearer example of the way in which a single pattern for a simple declarative sentence may be imposed through a sequence of entries. The sort of declarative sentence is obvious: simple but laden with subordinate clauses, many of them requiring an understood if.

iii. 20: This sizable entry now is to be subdivided, since some of the sentences are simple and smooth, and others contain a duplicated subject. 19:5A, A bed which was ..., and to which one ... -- the whole thing is ...; 19:6A, A bed to which one ..., and the corpse touched them -- they are unclean ... By contrast 19:7: A box, the opening of which is ... is susceptible to ... The same applies at 19:8A, 19:9A, 19:10A, and, ignoring the lo, these, at 20:1A, 20:2A, 20:3A, 20:4A, 20:5A (if understood throughout); 20:6A, 20:7A. Accordingly, the commencement of each principal cognitive unit, excluding the two opening ones, does carefully adhere to a single formulary pattern, the declarative sentence bearing a subordinated adjectival clause for the subject of the sentence. These are hardly routine or random occurrences.

iii. 21: The pattern at iii. 20 is carried forward with astonishing consistency. I do not think we need doubt that the two intermediate divisions are distinct from one another -- not merely separated by the accident of the intrusion of Chapter Twenty-One.

iii. 22: The common formula, All utensils have ..., should not obscure the still more strikingly consistent sentence-structure throughout, which is extended declarative sentences, as specified. 25:4-5 obviously are a separate unit, formulated in their own terms and obviously are a separate unit, formulated in their own terms and inserted whole. (The exegetical problems of that unit appear to be solved by reading the whole as entirely separate form the larger redactional-thematic context and inserted without regard to the principles of the remainder.)

iii. 24: He-who-apocopation.

iii. 25: Here we have a clearcut pattern, X which is ..., and which one put ..., is ... + apodosis, so 28:5A, 6A.

Ohalot

iii. 26: Even though we have a common theme and the common form of the declarative sentence, it is clear that the sentences are, among themselves, differentiable by their redaction preferences. 2:1A, 3A, 4, and 5 obviously comprise a unit unto themselves, building upon a contrastive predicate. 3:3F-G-5 form a dependent subunit of their own, for the reasons given.

iii. 27: While the dominant form is disputes, the disputes themselves yield simple declarative sentences, X (singular or plural), plain or with adjectival clauses, is/are unclean/clean. The shift from the redaction preference, the contrastive apodosis, of 2:5, is noteworthy and clear. Once more, therefore, we observe how the declarative sentence may itself yield extensive formalization, even when it consists of subject + verb + complement.

iii 29: The important issue here is whether all that unites 5:1-4 is the presence of Houses' disputes, which is to say, the shared apodosis. The answer is that the protasis also exhibits acute formalization:

5:1   An oven which ..., and the eye of which ..., and the cortege overshadowed it ...

5:2   A hatchway which is ..., and which a pot is placed ..., and it [the pot] is ...

(5:3   [If] it was whole -- continues the foregoing.)

(5:4   Appended.)

Accordingly, the protasis exhibits a striking formalization. Not only do we have a complex statement of the subject, an oven which ... and the eye of which ..., matched by a hatchway which ..., and on which a pot ..., but also the protasis further contains a duplicated subject in its third clause, and the cortege overshadowed ..., and it is ..., both modify a subordinated element of the antecedent adjectival clause. That is very solid evidence of acute formalization.

iii. 31: 7:3 consists of simple sentences, requiring an understood if. 7:4 shifts to he-who-apocopation. 7:5 continues 7:4. 7:6 reverts to he-who-apocopation. Accordingly, the unit is somewhat more diverse than earlier suggested, and its subgroup, 7:4-6, is clearly demarcated by a common formulary pattern not shared by 7:3. The way in which the whole was put together, and the reasons for its redaction, are clear.

iii. 32: The protasis of the Houses' disputes require an understood if at 11:4-6, in which case they form a coherent pattern.

iii. 34: Here we have he-who-apocopation at the outset, then the duplicated subject. The use of the duplicated subject for statements of measure is consistent and striking.

iii. 35: The declarative sentences share a preference for simple exposition, without adjectival encumbrances and subordinate clauses of any kind. It should be noted that a further unitary trait is the recurrence of the particular subject-matter of the subdivision, the projection.

iii. 40: Further examination of this extended unit confirms the original observation that we have a single formulary pattern, consisting of simple sentences with a subject, verb and complement (as required), with subordinate clauses, adjectival or otherwise, used very sparingly. If the bulk of Mishnah looked like this unit, we could hardly claim to have a document subjected to formalization and characterized by highly disciplined formulary patterns. I am unable to discern any significant, distinctive traits in this long inter-mediate division of simple declarative sentences, even though, as noted, a few subunits do fall together. Among these are 16:3A, he who, 16:4, he who, 17:1, He who ploughs ..., 17:2 [If] one was ploughing, 17:3 He who ploughs; 17:4-5, SDH HPRS, 17:5, SDH S ...; 18;2-4, an obviously unitary construction; and so on. Nonetheless, I do not know why, if we have such patterned units, we are unable to discern important traits of syntactical formalization, which I have found so characteristic in the bulk of our materials.

Negaim

iii. 41: Of course we again discern obvious primary redactional units in this sizable intermediate division. 1:1, expanded by 1:2, is hardly comparable to 1:3-6, which constitute a subunit of obvious balance and internal discipline. The declarative sentences at 2:1-3:5, by contrast, do consist of subject + verb + complement, a long sequence of simple rules, simply stated. 2:1, 2, 3, 4, and 5 share a preference for R'H, but that seems to me required by the substance of the rule. 2:5 and 3:1 are joined by KL, not much of a union. On merely formulary grounds, we should be hard put to distinguish the closing subdivision of Ohalot from the opening subdivision of Negaim.

iii. 47: The principal building blocks are 9:1A and 9:2A, The boil and burning are made unclean ..., The boil and burning are not made unclean ... The units of 9:2 certainly constitute a unitary construction.

iii. 49: This subdivision exactly follows the model of the foregoing. The two intermediate divisions together exhibit the disciplined formalization which, seen separately, they do not clearly indicate.

iii. 50-52. Once more we find a vast sequence of declarative sentences, distinguished as subdivisions only by the shift in subject or theme. Let us now distinguish among the many sorts of sentences in accord with the principal categories established earlier.

A. Subject + verb + predicate

11:1A-C, E, F-J; 11:3A, B-C, D, E; 11:4D, E, F-H + I; 11:6A-C, C-D (if understood); 11:8A; 11:8D-G, H-I; 11:10A-B, C, D, E, F-H; 11:11A + B-E; 11:11H, I.

12:1A, C, D; 12:2A-C, D, E, F + 12:3A-H; 12:4A-C, D-E (matched); 12:4F, G; 12:5A + B (Scripture), C + D (Scripture), E, F, G (speech); 12:6A + B (Scripture), C + D-E (Scripture), F, G (matched), + H, I-L.

13:1A-T (internally coherent formulary pattern); 13:3F-G, H, I, J + K; 13:4A, B, C; 13:5A-C, D-F + F; 13:7A-B, C-D + E (+ F + G) (matched); 13:10A-C, D-F (+ G) (matched); 13:12A-B + C, D-E (matched).

14:1A-B, C, D, E, F-G, H; 14:2A, B, C, D, E, F; 14:3A, B, C-I (unitary + matched); 14:4; 14:5E, F + G, H-I (matched), J, K; 14:6 (unitary) A = D, B = D; 14:7A, B; 14:8A, B, C, D, E, F + G; 14:9A, B, C + D, E-G; 14:10A-B, C, D, E, F-G (Scripture), H + I-K, L-M, N-O (matched); 14:12A-B (matched), C + D-E.

B. Duplicated Subject

11:2A-E + E; 11:5A, B, C, D-F, G-H, I-J + K-L; 11:7H; 11-8B, C.

13:2A-B + C, D.

14:5A-B, C (+ D).

C. Contrastive Predicate: None

D. He-Who-Apocopation

11:1C-D; 11:4A-C; 11:6F-G + H-J; 11:7A-C (+ C-G); 11:9A-G + H-J; 11:11F-G; 11:12A-B (+ C), D-E (+ F).

12:1B.

13:2D-I, 13:3A-C + D-E; 13:6A-D + E; 13:11A-B + C-F.

14:11A-B + C, 14:13 A-D + E.

We see that while, in the main, we have declarative sentences, these in fact are to be distinguished from one another, and the principal distinction among diverse sentences consisting of subject + verb + object is that groups of sentences will be matched in construction with one another. It must once again be stressed, therefore, that syntactical formalization solely serves as a gross category, within which is a considerable range of possibilities. Let me state the upshot with emphasis: Formalization thus is accomplished among simple declarative sentences primarily by matching one sentence in a cognitive unit against another. That should be regarded as itself evidence of the highly formal character even of the (seemingly random) declarative sentences thus set into patterned balance with one another.

Parah

iii. 54: While the form is the dispute, the formulary pattern common to the protasis + stich of the apodosis is the simple declarative sentence, subject + predicate, e.g., A cow used for purification which is pregnant is fit/unfit. It is/is not purchased ...

iii. 55: Here the differentiation among the declarative sentences is achieved through noting the use of present, continuous, plural participles as against singular past tense verb-forms. The division then is 3:1-6 as against 3:8-11 (Part IX, pp. 44-47). The differentiation which is thereby accomplished is both formal and substantive. It is to be discerned not in the individual cognitive units but among the formulation of several sets thereof, as above, iii. 50:52.

iii. 56: The sentences are smooth. 4:1A-F is rich in qualificatory clauses formed of verbs, and the remainder of 4:1 and 4:2-3 likewise exhibit a marked preference for or-clauses (with or understood).

iii. 57: The several declarative sentences fall into the following formal units: 5:1-2, He-who + smoothly appended predicate; 5:3-4, That which, duplicated subject, 5:5 then does reveal the shift as noted above, since the sentences now are complete and simple, normally without a duplicated subject. 5:7 follows this same pattern; 5:6 is a simple sentence, X is fit. 5:8 has a duplicated subject, and 5:9 is built on he-who-apocopation. In all, as noted above, the set from 5:5 to 5:9 is not joined by formal coherence. But the several forms used therein are familiar and routine, not random.

iii. 60: The pattern is as stated above, He who does so and so does such and such or is such and such. There is no apocopation whatsoever, and the common formulary trait is pronounced.

iii. 61: The sentences of this unit follow the established pattern, subject + verb + complement or subject + smoothly joined predicate.

iii. 62: Here we may certainly not distinguish one group of declarative sentences from another. All we have are subject and suitable predicates, lacking significant syntactical differentiation. Yet when we examine the unit by itself, we do see patterns internal to its sentences, e.g., 10:1, Whatever is suitable to become unclean ... Whatever is suitable to become unclean; 10:2, he who is clean for ..., he who is clean for ..., so to 10:4A. 10:4B commences a sequence, [If] one was standing ... The internal unity of 10:6 is obvious.

iii. 63: The declarative sentences exhibit no syntactical variety. What unites the set and distinguishes it from others is, of course, the recurrence of its key-word, hyssop.

iii. 64: The differentiation among the types of declarative sentences is worked out above.

Tohorot

iii. 66: Once more we observe that internal to a series of cognitive units, all of them forming mere "simple declarative sentences," will be internal balance, the formation of matched declarative sentences. Simply stating that we have a subject, verb and complement or a subject and predicate, closely tied to one another, should not obscure the many and diverse ways by which a sequence of cognitive units will follow a single pattern, such as is internal to M. 3:1-3. There can be no doubt, because of the presence of an apophthegmatic phrase linking the set, that the several units are formulated in close correlation to one another.

iii. 67: The unifying element is the use of NMS', 3:6, 7, and 8, and, accordingly, the introductory unit, 3:5, with its stress on MS', is integral to the whole. Once more, the use of the simple declarative sentence is secondary to the redactional plan for the whole intermediate division.

iii. 71: It is solely the recurrently understood if [or if there is] which can be seen to mark the declarative sentences of this subdivision.

iii. 73: Here we have subunits at 6:5, if understood; 6:6A-B matched by C-D, thus a pericope made up of internally balanced sentences; and 6:6 Dff., in which the operative unifying phrase is "private domain for the Sabbath and public domain for uncleanness," 6:6G, I, 6:7C, E, 6:8B, D-E, and 6:9B, E, and F. Once again the declarative sentences are unified in sizable groups by recurrent formulary patterns or word-choices internal to the conception which is to be formulated.

iii. 75: The disputes yield more than a single sort of syntactical construction. 9:1 is a duplicated subject. The sentences of 9:2-3 have in common the implied if. 9:4, 5, and 6 all begin with he-who, followed by a tightly rejoined predicate, thus a subunit of the subdivision. 9:7 builds on the understood if.

iii. 76: 9:8-9. This unitary subdivision rests upon the topic of 9:8, The dead creeping thing which is found of 9:8A, understood at 9:9A.

Miqvaot

iii. 84: Let us characterize the kinds of declarative sentences found at 6:1-11.

6:1A constitutes a declarative sentence, conceptually continued by the remainder of its cognitive unit. 6:1B-C contains a duplicated subject, and its syntax is followed and matched at 6:1D and by extension, F-G. 6:2A-B likewise have a duplicated subject.

6:3A-H + I form a long but relatively smooth sentence, with many understood if's.

6:4 yields a complete declarative sentence, "The sponge and bucket which contained and [which] fell ..., have not rendered it ...."

6:5A-B present a that-which-apocopated sentence, with the rest of its cognitive unit in simple sentences.

6:6A-C follow the pattern of 6:4.

6:7A is a simple declarative sentence, so too 6:8A-C, 6:9A, and 6:10A-C. Accordingly, the construction as a whole contains declarative sentences of various kinds, with some clearcut subunits which accord with one or another familiar pattern.

iii. 90: 10:1A-B is a richly augmented declarative sentence. The qualifying phrases of A-D then are resumed at G. 10:2A is matched by B and generalized at C. 10:3-4 form a matched pair. 10:5A returns to 10:1A, but now with a duplicated subject. 10:5D is matched at E in what looks to be a contrastive predicate. 10:6C is matched at D and E. 10:7 contains two matched sentences, syllable for syllable, at A and B, then concluded at C-D. 10:8A-C is matched by D-E, with the same form at F-G and H-I.

Here the recognition of the limits of the subdivision should not obscure that the units of which the subdivision is composed are themselves formulated in terms of familiar, disciplined patterns. But the redaction of the subdivision is separate and distinct from the formulation of its components, and this is not common in our present exercise.

Niddah

iii. 92: Like general rules on the uncleanness of plagues and general rules on the rules for burning the red cow, here too we find simple declarative sentences, which state simple rules on the uncleanness of the menstruating woman. There is a contrastive subject at 2:1A, a unit continued at 2:2 and 2:3. That means we have to refer back to 2:1 for the match to 2:4, KL. 2:5 is sui generis. 2:6-7 obviously form a prior redactional unit.

iii. 94: The redactional link is not only the use of the declarative sentence, but the recurrence of BNWT at 4:1A and 4:2A. 4:3 continues in theme and, in a general way, in the formulary pattern.

iii. 97: 5:9 is a set of closely matched declarative sentences, in which the same units recur in one sentence after another. 6:1 continues 5:9. 6:11 is like 5:9, in that each of its elements is matched in form and conception. 6:12 continues 6:11. Accordingly, as we have observed, even when the characteristic pattern is the simple declarative sentence, the units themselves exhibit care at the use of formalized patterns internal to their cognitive limits, matched by the immediately adjacent units.

iii. 98: The subunits of this immense subdivision are specified above and do not require further discussion. It is clear that the intermediate division -- if it is properly set aside as an intermediate division! -- is made up of several subunits, each of them carefully composed in disciplined patterns.

Makhshirin

iii. 101: 2:1A and B present contrastive subjects. 2:1C, D, and E are matched. 2:2A-B present a contrastive predicate. 2:2C-E are in standard apocopation, as are 2:3A-D, both sets being matched with the common traits of a duplicated subject and contrastive predicate.

iii. 102: Here we have he-who-apocopation at 4:6A-B + C-E, 4:6F-G + H, 4:7A-C + D. Then 4:8A-C form a simple, declarative sentence, with necessary qualificatory language. 4:9 reverts to he-who-apocopation. 4:10A-B is matched at C, D. 5:1A-B,

5:2A-B, 5:3A + B or C, 5:4A-C, 5:5A-B, and 6:5A-C, all yield the familiar he-who-apoco-pation. It follows that the simple declarative sentences in this set are formally subor-dinate to its principal formulary preference.

iii. 109: Once more, general rules on contamination, now regarding the Zab, are contained in simple declarative sentences. The inner construction of 2:1-4 is explained at Part XVIII, p. 30-40: formally implicit or explicit lists.

iii. 111: The declarative sentences of this unit are spelled out above. The patterns are by no means discrete and random.

Tebul Yom

iii. 114: 1:3, 1:4, and 1:5 all begin with lists of several items followed by a tightly-joined predicate.

Yadayim

iii. 116: It is by now not surprising that general rules on washing hands are given in simple sequences of declarative sentences, They do this, they do that, predominant at 1:1, 2, 2:3, 1:3 and 1:5 begin with, The water which, and 1:4, with an implied if, depends on 1:3. 2:1 and 2:2 likewise require an understood if.

iii. 118: What links the entries of this set together is the common predicate, impart uncleanness to hands. 3:3, 3:4, 3:5, and 4:5 are consistent in listing items to which the predicate is added without variation.

Uqsin

iii. 120: Once more we find a common predicate, receive uncleanness, impart uncleanness, join together, 2:2A, 2:4A. 2:5's predicate is HBWR. The several units, as is clear upon examination, are internally unified by repeated patterns such as the recurrent predicate. I do not see a substantial and important common formulary trait among these several sentences, but, as is clear, each has been constructed with care.

iii. 134: Once more the distinguishing trait is not only the declarative sentence but the recurrent predicate, here, is made unclean as food.

iv. Conclusion

We may now answer the question with which this substantial exercise opens. The principal framework of formulation and formalization in the Mishnah clearly is the intermediate division rather than the cognitive unit. Exceptions to this rule are those subdivisions in which no clearcut formulary pattern, other than the "simple declarative sentence" without qualification, characterizes the several component, cognitive units. Otherwise, we observe, the least-formalized formulary pattern, the simple declarative sentence, turns out to yield many examples of acute formalization, in which a single distinctive pattern is imposed upon two or more cognitive units. While we see that an intermediate division of a tractate may be composed of several such conglomerates of cognitive units, we also observe that it is rare indeed for cognitive units formally to stand wholly by themselves. Normally, though not invariably, cognitive units share formal or formulary traits with others to which they are juxtaposed and the theme of which they share. It follows, as I said, that the principal unit of formulary formalization is the intermediate division and not the cognitive unit.

The bulk of the work of giving expression to the cognitive units therefore is carried out in the processes of redaction which resulted in the formation -- patterning and aggregation -- of the intermediate divisions of the several tractates -- in their formulation, and, it is obvious, in their organization and thematic arrangement. The Mishnah is the work of tradent-redactors. The mnemonic consists of the confluence of topic and rhetoric at the level of deep logic, as I said in the preface.

It remains to observe that the redactional and formulary traits of the Tosefta are strikingly different from those of the Mishnah. When we find in the Tosefta patterns deemed syntactically distinctive, they generally are in pericopae which depend for meaning and form on the Mishnah. When we find Toseftan pericopae in which close attention is paid to matters of formulary patterning, they tend to constitute autonomous pericopae, relevant, but merely supplementary, to the Mishnah. The net result is that the redactional and formulary traits of the Mishnah are distinctive to the Mishnah and materials which, from one perspective or another, might find a comfortable place in the Mishnah, which is to say, materials in no way formulated as a commentary to the Mishnah but given patterns of their own.

CHAPTER FOUR
FROM MNEMONICS TO MEANING IN THE MISHNAH

i. Formulation and Transmission of the Mishnah: The Mnemonic Fact

The dominant stylistic trait of the Mishnah is the acute formalization of its syntactical structure, specifically, its intermediate divisions, so organized that the limits of a theme correspond to those of a formulary pattern. The balance and order of the Mishnah are particular to the Mishnah. Tosefta does not sustainedly reveal equivalent traits. Since the Mishnah is so very distinctive a document, we now investigate the intentions of the people who made it. About whom does it speak? And why, in particular, have its authorities distinctively shaped language, which in the Tosefta does not speak in rhymes and balanced, matched declarative sentences, imposing, upon the conceptual, factual prose of the law, a peculiar kind of poetry? Why do they create rhythmic order, grammatically balanced sentences containing discrete laws, laid out in what seem to be carefully enumerated sequences, and the like? Language not only contains culture, which could not exist without it. Language -- in our case, linguistic and syntactical style and stylization -- expresses a world-view and ethos. Whose world-view is contained and expressed in the Mishnah's formalized rhetoric?

In the discussion which follows I make no reference whatsoever to the similarly stylized and formalized modes of expression in other documents of law or religion, in ancient times and later on. Self-evidently, the traits of stylization to which I allude are not distinctive to the Mishnah, except in its own context. Davis Mellinkoff, The Language of Law (Boston, 1963) points to many traits of legal language which will be familiar to readers of this work, e.g., distinctive use of a common language for a particular purpose, the presence of mannerisms of various kinds, formal words and expressions, and the like. Literary traits of documents much closer to the Mishnah in time upon examination appear to be not distant from the Mishnah's. Remarkably reminiscent of Sifra, the Pahlavi Nirangestan, for example, presents citations of Avesta followed by something very like pericopae in dispute-form, a statement of a problem, with diverse opinions, in the names of authorities + guft (= 'WMR) + balanced and matched opinions. My interpretation of the relationship between Mishnaic rhetorical patterns and the reality contained and expressed therein and of the larger meaning of that rhetoric is directed wholly and completely to the document at hand and to the system of which it is a principal expression. It is by no means meant to exclude the possibility that similar literary preferences in other systems and their literature generate exactly the same approach to the interpretation of the meaning of those preferences, or the possibility that exactly the same literary traits bear wholly other meanings in other systems. My claim in all that follows is that Mishnaic redactional and formal traits are to be interpreted, in this context, as expressions of the Mishnaic world and testimonies to its conceptions of reality. Systemic interpretation is all that is attempted here. A more wide-ranging and comparative approach certainly is of interest. But since exactly the same phenomenon may, in diverse systems, bear quite various meanings, the comparative approach must be to systems, not to matters of detail. The problem of undertaking the requisite comparison for me is that I know no work equivalent to mine in the systematic exposition of the laws, system, and language of rules of uncleanness, e.g., of the Pahlavi code.

To return to the main point: there is no reason to doubt that if we asked the tradental-redactional authorities behind the Mishnah the immediate purpose of their formalization, their answer would be, to facilitate memorization. For that is the proximate effect of the acute formalization of their document. Much in its character can be seen as mnemonic. The Mishnah was not published in writing, Lieberman (cited above) maintains: "Since in the entire Talmudic literature we do not find that a book of the Mishnah was ever consulted in the case of controversies or doubt concerning a particular reading, we may safely conclude that the compilation was not published in writing, that a written ekdosis [edition] of the Mishnah did not exist."

The Mishnah was published in a different way: "A regular oral ekdosis, edition, of the Mishnah was in existence, a fixed text recited by the Tannaim of the college. The Tanna ("repeater," reciter) committed to memory the text of certain portions of the Mishnah which he subsequently recited in the college in the presence of the great masters of the Law. Those Tannaim were pupils chosen for their extraordinary memory, although they were not always endowed with due intelligence ... When the Mishnah was committed to memory and the Tannaim recited it in the college, it was thereby published and possessed all the traits and features of a written ekdosis ... Once the Mishnah was accepted among the college Tannaim (reciters) it was difficult to cancel it." Lieberman's evidence for these conclusions is drawn from two sources, first, sayings within the rabbinical corpus and stories about how diverse problems of transmission of materials were worked out, second, parallels, some of them germane but none of them probative, drawn from Greco-Roman procedures of literary transmission.

Considerably more compelling evidence of the same proposition derives from the internal character of the Mishnah itself. But if stylization and formalization testify to a mnemonic program, then absence of the same traits must mean that some materials were not intended to be memorized. The Mishnah, and the the Mishnah alone, was the corpus to be formulated for memorization and transmitted through 'living books,' Tannaim, to the coming generations. The Tosefta cannot have been formulated along the same lines. Accordingly, the Mishnah is given a special place and role by those who stand behind it.

We have seen the marks of a remarkably coherent, cogent, and exceedingly limited corpus of literary-formulaic devices and redactional conventions. We have been wholly unable to point to significant divergence from a single norm of agglutination: reliance upon distinctive formulary traits which are imposed on a sequence of sentences, and upon distinctive thematic substance, expressed by these same patterned sentences. That is now intermediate units were put together and accounts also for the formalization of small ones -- without reference to the diversity of authorities cited therein. As I said, four distinctive syntactical patterns characterize all, with the fifth, the "simple declarative sentence" itself so shaped as to yield its own distinctive traits. If there are traces of diverse theories of formulation and redaction of materials in our division, which would reflect the individual preferences and styles of diverse circles over two hundred years, we have not found them. Those who maintain that the Mishnah as we know it not merely contains ideas from successive generations but also preserves the language and whole sequences of pericopae made up by these successive generations will want to specify the criteria for the recognition of the diverse literary results of those divergent groups.

The unified and cogent formal character of the Mishnah testifies in particular to that of its ultimate tradent-redactors. We learn in the Mishnah about the intention of that last generation of Mishnaic authorities, who gave us the document as we have it. It is their way of saying things which we know for certain. From this we hope to learn something about them and their world-view. One certain fact is that they choose to hand on important materials in such a form as facilitated memorization. The second, which follows closely, is that the document is meant to be memorized. Whether or not it also was copied and transmitted in writing, and whether or not such copies were deemed authoritative, are not questions we can answer on the basis of the Mishnah's internal evidence. The Tosefta certainly suggests that the Mishnah-pericopae were copied and glossed, but its evidence does not pertain to these larger issues.

ii. Rhetoric and Reality

It follows that the system of grammar and syntax distinctive to the Mishnah expresses rules and conventions intelligible to members of a particular community, that which stands behind the Mishnah. It certainly is a peculiar kind of formalized language. It is formed to facilitate a principal function, memorization and transmission of special rules. The language of the Mishnah therefore does not relate those who made and used it to one another or to the world in which they lived. It is not a functional instrument of neutral communication. Rather, it distinguishes its users from that ordinary world, and sets apart one aspect of their interrelationships, the one defined in the Mishnah, from such other aspects as do not require speech in a few patterns and in a kind of poetry. Accordingly, while the language represented in part by the Mishnah may or may not have been used for other purposes than those defined by the Mishnah, the way in which that language is used in the Mishnah bespeaks a limited and circumscribed circumstance. How things were said can have been grasped primarily by the people instructed in saying and hearing things in just that way. In this sense formalized language sets the Mishnah apart from its larger linguistic context, for Middle Hebrew was a language utilized outside of rabbinical circles.

The Mishnah's is language for an occasion. The occasion is particular: formation and transmission of special sorts of conceptions in a special way. The predominant, referential function of language, which is to give verbal structure to the message itself, is secondary in our document. The expressive function, to convey the speaker's attitude toward what he is talking about, the conative function, to focus upon <u>who</u> is being addressed, and other ritualized functions of language come to the fore. The Mishnah's language, as I said, therefore is special, meant as an expression of a non-referential function (Farb, <u>Word Play</u>, pp. 23-24). So far as the Mishnah was meant to be memorized by a particular group of people for a distinctive purpose, it is language which includes few and excludes many, unites those who use it and sets them apart from others who do not.

The formal rhetoric of the Mishnah is empty of content, which is proved by the fact that pretty much all themes and conceptions can be reduced to these same few formal patterns. These patterns, I have shown, are established by syntactical recurrences, as distinct from repetition of sounds. The same words do not recur, except in the case of the few forms we have specified, or key-words in a few contexts. These forms have to be excised from the formulary patterns in which they occur, e.g., 'WMR, M^CSH, the dispute, so that we may discern the operative and expressive patterns themselves. On the other hand, long sequences of sentences fail to repeat the same words -- that is, syllabic balance, rhythm, or sound -- yet they do establish a powerful claim to order and formulary sophistication and perfection. That is why we could name a pattern, <u>he-who</u> ... <u>it is</u> ...-apocopation: The arrangement of the words, as a grammatical pattern, not their substance, is indicative of pattern. Accordingly, while we have a document composed along what clearly are mnemonic lines, <u>the document's susceptibility to memorization rests principally upon the utter abstraction of recurrent syntactical patterns, rather than on the concrete repetition of particular words, rhythms, syllabic counts, or sounds.</u>

A sense for the deep, inner logic of word-patterns, of grammar and syntax, rather than for their external similarities, governs the Mishnaic mnemonic. Even though the Mishnah is to be memorized and handed on orally, it expresses a mode of thought attuned to abstract relationships, rather than concrete and substantive forms. The formulaic, not the formal, character of Mishnaic rhetoric yields a picture of a subculture which speaks of immaterial and not material things. In this subculture the relationship, rather than the thing or person which is related, is primary and constitutes the principle of reality. The thing in itself is less than the thing in cathexis with other things, so too the person. The repetition of form creates form. But what here is repeated is not form, but formulary pattern, a pattern effected through persistent grammatical or syntactical relationships and affecting an infinite range of diverse objects and topics. Form and structure emerge not from concrete, formal things but from abstract and unstated, but ubiquitous and powerful relationships.

This fact -- the creation of pattern through grammatical relationship of syntactical elements, more than through concrete sounds -- tells us that the people who memorized conceptions reduced to these particular forms were capable of extraordinarily abstract perception. Hearing peculiarities of word-order in quite diverse cognitive contexts, their ears and minds perceived regularities of grammatical arrangement, repeated functional variations of utilization of diverse words, grasping from such subtleties syntactical patterns not imposed or expressed by recurrent external phenomena and autonomous of particular meanings. What they heard, it is clear, not only were abstract relationships, but also principles conveyed along with and through these relationships. For what was memorized, as I have said, was a fundamental notion, expressed in diverse examples but in recurrent rhetorical-syntactical patterns. Accordingly, what they could and did hear was what lay far beneath the surface of the rule: both the unstated principle and the unsounded pattern. This means, I stress, that their mode of thought was attuned to what lay beneath the surface, their mind and their ears perceived what was not said behind what was said, and how it was said. Social interrelationships within the community of Israel are left behind in the ritual speech of the Mishnah, just as, within the laws, natural realities are made to give form and expression to supernatural or metaphysical regularities. The Mishnah speaks of Israel, but the speakers are a group apart. The Mishnah talks of this-worldly things, but the things stand for and evoke another world entirely.

Who is the personna, serving as the Mishnah's voice? The Mishnah is remarkably indifferent to the identification and establishment of the character of the person who speaks. It not only is formally anonymous, in that it does not bear a signature or a single first-person identification. It also is substantively anonymous, in that it does not permit variation of patterns of formulation to accord with the traits of individuals or even to suggest that individuals who do occur have distinctive traits of speech, word-choice, or, in the final analysis, even generative conception. This absence of individuation should not suggest that the Mishnah to our Division is essentially neutral as to the imposition of a highly distinctive mode of discourse. The contrary is the case. Green (Biography) states this matter as follows:

These documents appear to be not accidental, inchoate collections, but carefully and deliberately constructed compilations. Each document has its own ideological and theological agendum, and it is axiomatic that the agendum of any document, though shaped to a degree by inherited materials, ultimately is the creation of the authorities, most of whom are anonymous, who produced the document itself. They have determined the focus, selected the materials, and provided the framework that unites the discrete pericopae and gives the document its internal consistency and coherence. The features of these documents suggest that their agenda transcend the teaching of any single master.

First, rabbinic documents contain a substantial amount of unattributed material. This gives them an atemporal quality, and creates the sense that the document, or the tradition, is speaking for itself, independent of any individual mind.

Second, rabbinic documents are not constructed around the sayings of any individual, but follow either a thematic, formal, topical, or scriptural arrangement in which the teachings of opinions of various masters are gathered together to address a single issue or to interpret a particular verse of scripture. This sort of arrangement points to a process of selection in which the teachings of individuals have been made subservient to the goals of the documents. Indeed, within the documents the comments of the masters and their disagreements with each other almost always focus on matters of detail. The larger conceptions which inform the documents themselves are never called into question ...

Third, although every teaching in rabbinic literature originated in the mind of an individual, the continued vitality of those teachings depended on the rabbinic circles and communities who preserved and transmitted them. The chain of tradents, only occasionally mentioned by name, the redactors and the editors who stand behind the present form of both discrete pericopae and entire documents substantively revised, embellished and defined received materials, and sometimes invented new ones, to suit their various agenda.

All of this means that we know about early rabbinic figures what the various authorities behind the documents want us to know, and we know it in the way they wanted us to know it. Consequently, the historical context, the primary locus of interpretation for any saying attributed to a given master or story about him is the document in which the passage appears, not the period in which he is alleged to have lived.

What does the rhetoric of the Mishnah leave unstated? The first thing we never are told is who is speaking, where we are, and the purpose for which discourse is undertaken. These may be taken for granted, but nothing in the Mishnah of our Division and little enough in the Tosefta cares to tell us about the societal or concrete context of rhetoric. If this is a mode of communication, then to whom is communication addressed? Who, we ask again, is the speaker, and who the listener?

The sole evidence of the speaker is the use of the invariable attributive. 'WMR, which bears no meaning particular to a saying and homogenizes all sayings. 'WMR states only that what follows bears the name of an authority and therefore is claimed to be authoritative. 'WMR is all we are told about the setting of a saying, where it was said, for what purpose, and, in all, in what social, spatial, temporal, and intellectual context. To put matters simply, 'WMR obscures all data of particularity and human circumstance. Yet 'WMR generally, though not always, is intellectually partitive. That is, once we have the presence of 'WMR, we know that a private authority, not the anonymous and unanimous consensus of the corpus represented by the speaker -- the document -- is at hand. The use of 'WMR establishes that the conception now to be stated is private. No claim is to be made for the consensus of the community for what is to be said. It follows that the silence of the Mishnah on the authority behind a saying means to claim the consensus of the community (to speak in solely secular terms) for the stated proposition.

But is what is stated to be interpreted as transactional, in that relationships between speaker, listener, and topic are presupposed? The Mishnah is remarkably reticent on that very matter. Its language invariably is descriptive, in the continuous participle. Its claim, through formal rhetoric, is that such-and-so is the way things are, describes and establishes the norms and forms of being. There is no speaker nor person-spoken-to, in the sense that a single individual to some other gives private expression to what is said (whether it reflects consensus of private opinion) or private context to what is heard. The acute formalization of all things detaches from the private person any claim that he alone says, in his own way, a particular opinion. It imposes upon all sayings the authority of the document as a whole (again, to use secular and descriptive language). The absence of differentiation among, and description of, the audience to what is said bears the same implication. This is how things are, without regard to the situation to which they are addressed, the condition, let alone opinion, of the people by whom they are heard. The abstraction of thought is carried over into the nuanced situation of the people by whom and to whom thought is conveyed.

In this sense, therefore, the language of the Mishnah and its grammatically formalized rhetoric create a world of discourse quite separate from the concrete realities of a given time, place, or society. The exceedingly limited repertoire of grammatical patterns by which all things on all matters are said gives symbolic expression to the notion that beneath the accidents of life are a few, comprehensive relationships: <u>unchanging and enduring patterns lie deep in the inner structure of reality and impose structure upon the accidents of the world.</u> This means, as I have implied, that reality for the Mishnaic rhetoric consists in the grammar and syntax of language, consistent and enduring patterns of relationship among diverse and changing concrete things or persons. What lasts is not the concrete thing but the abstract interplay governing any and all sorts of concrete things. There is, therefore a congruence between rhetorical patterns of speech, on the one side, and the framework of discourse established by these same patterns, on the other. Just as we accomplish memorization by perceiving not what is said but how what is said is persistently arranged, so we speak to, undertake to address and describe, a world in which what is concrete and material is secondary. The mode of expression in all contexts is principal.

The Mishnah's ideas are shaped, in particular, as gnomic expressions. They deal with basic truths, make use of devices to create a pattern (if not one of sound). The vocabulary is invariably impersonal, <u>they do</u> or <u>one does</u> or <u>he who</u>. And the verb nearly always is in the present tense, and always is in the present tense for descriptive rules. This too enhances the aura of universal application. So too, "Constructions such as parallelism, symmetry, and reversal of the elements in the expression are common" (Farb, <u>Word Play</u>, p. 118). Farb states, "These characteristics combine to produce a strategy of language manipulation for the particular purposes of teaching, conveying wisdom, and expressing a philosophy." (Farb, p. 118). But all of this is attained, as we have seen, through formalization of syntax at its deep levels.

The skill of the formulators of the Mishnah is to manipulate the raw materials of everyday speech. What they have done is so to structure language as to make it strange and alien, to impose a fresh perception upon what to others -- and what in the Tosefta -- are merely unpatterned and ordinary ways of saying things. What is said in the Mishnah is simple. How it is said is arcane. Ordinary folk cannot have had much difficulty understanding the words, which refer to ordinary actions and objects. How long it must have taken to grasp the meaning of the patterns into which the words are arranged, how hard it was and is to do so, is suggested by the necessity for the creation of Tosefta, the two Talmuds, and the commentaries in the long centuries since the Mishnah came into being. In this sense, the Mishnah speaks openly about public matters, yet its deep substructure of syntax and grammatical forms shapes what is said into an essentially ritualistic language. It takes many years to master the difficult argot, though only a few minutes to memorize the simple patterns. That paradox reflects the situation of the creators of the Mishnah.

Up to now I have said only a little about tense structure. The reason is that the Mishnah exhibits remarkable indifference to the potentialities of meaning inherent therein. Its persistent preference for the plural participle, thus the descriptive present tense, is matched by its capacity to accept the mixture of past, present, and future tenses, which can be jumbled together in a single sentence and, even more commonly, in a single pericope. It follows that the Mishnah is remarkably uninterested in differentiation of time-sequences. This fact is most clearly shown by the gemisch of the extreme-apocopated sentence, with its capacity to support something like the following: "He who does so and so ... the rain came and wet it down ... if he was happy ... it [is] Under the law, If water be put." Clearly, the matter of tense, past, present, future, is simply not relevant to the purpose of the speaker. If tense is irrelevant, however, then we find ourselves in the undifferentiated present. What is said is meant to bear no relationship whatever to the circumstance or particular time or context in which what is said applies. The absence of a powerful and recurrent system of tense-differentiation is strong evidence in favor of our conception that the Mishnah describes a world detached from time.

The temporal and worldly authority of the Mishnah's unspecified "speaker" likewise is curiously unspecified. What is omitted is any reference to a system of institutional enforcement, political, or supernatural. At no point in our division is there an effort to give nuance to language to be used for one setting, as against some other, in the home as distinct from the Temple, the court, the school, or the street. The homogenization of thought and its expression in a limited and uniform rhetorical pattern impose the conception that the norms are axiomatic for, and expose the logic of, all situations in general, but pertain to none in particular. This once again brings to the surface the notion, implicit in the way the Mishnah says things, that the Mishnah describes how things are, whether or not material-reality conforms. The absence of descriptive reference to a speaker and his role reenforces the conception that this-worldly details of identified authorities, with circumscribed and concrete authority, are not pertinent. The reason is that what comes under description does not depend upon the details of this-worldly institutions. That is why the document is so strikingly indifferent to the differentiation of rhetoric. Diverse ideational materials are reduced to a single rhetoric. The various contexts to which what is said is applicable are never given specific definition in the choice of words or rhetorical patterns. In the profoundly conventional discourse of the Mishnah, the one thing left untouched by the affect of convention is the concrete world, which is to conform, whether in fact it does or does not conform.

It scarcely needs saying that this sameness of rhetoric hardly is functional to the situation of ordinary people. If the language of the Mishnah serves a small group, its intent is quite the opposite: to encompass and describe all things. We have therefore to distinguish between the effects of formalization of thought, which produce a private framework of discourse among specialists, and the function thereof, which is to make discourse among individuals public and general and abstract it from the ordinary life. The Mishnah lacks abundant ways to speak in grammatical utterances, reducing to its handful of possibilities all truths about all things pertinent to Purities (not to exclude the other five divisions). A level of address has been chosen, and, it is clear, is severely imposed upon all themes and all contexts. It is not possible for that aesthetic-mnemonic sameness to express the diverse things which need saying in ordinary circumstances.

In this sense the Mishnaic rhetoric, while anti-contextual, creates its own context of meaning. Its indifference to any other setting of discourse but its own is suggested, as I said, by its partitive attributional formula, the same for all sayings of one genre, and also by its single honorific. The Mishnah is remarkably uninterested in diverse honorifics, using the single title, Rabbi, in all circumstances and for nearly all named authorities. The some differentiation effected by the title is to omit from consideration the teachings of people who do not have that title, and this is effected solely in the Tosefta. As I said, the absence of all reference to who is listening imposes an equivalent sameness upon the audience. What is said is said to whom it may concern, and the important parts of what is said are stated by people who are permitted neither individuation nor identification, who talk, as I have emphasized, in the same syntactical patterns about all subjects and in all contexts. In context it is trivial to notice that sexual differences play no role, except as demanded by the setting of a case or rule. Since women do the cooking, cases and examples of rules which deal with kneading dough will use the feminine form. In general, though, in the Mishnah there is neither male nor female, nor is there the slightest suggestion that women speak differently from men. Where a woman is quoted, what she is made to say, hardly surprisingly, is in the familiar rhetoric. The reason is that differences of sex are as irrelevant to the Mishnah's speech-world as differences of context, social status, or institutional circumstance.

Outside of the precedents ($ma^c asim$), the formal characteristics of which are difficult to discern and which in any case occur seldom in the Mishnah, our Order presents remarkably little living dialogue. (X says is not dialogue, nor are disputes and debates dialogical in any natural sense.) Mishnaic syntax is based upon the monologue. Occasionally, as in disputes, two or more monologues are juxtaposed, but scarcely constitute dialogues. The reciter recites. No response is suggested within our document. In this sense, dialogue, a basic form human speech, is noteworthy for its absence. Tosefta makes up for the matter, with its citation of the Mishnah, as if to assume one side of a conversation, and its even more pronounced effort at interchange, its reference to something mentioned by the Mishnah in the form, "What are ...?" or "Under what circumstances ...?" But in the main the document's highly formal character precludes the possibility of dialogue, there being only a few ways of possibly uttering a thought, and these, as we have seen, not only formal but also gnomic.

The extraordinary lack of a context of communication -- specification of speaker, hearer -- of our document furthermore suggests that for the Mishnah, language is a self-contained formal system used more or less incidentally for communication. It is a system for description of a reality, the reality of which is created and contained by, and exhausted within, the description. The saying of the words, whether heard meaningfully by another or not, is the creation of the world. Speech is action and creation. The speech-community represented by the Mishnah stands strongly not only against nuance but also against change. The imposition of conventional and highly patterned syntax clearly is meant to preserve what is said without change (even though, we know, changes in the wording of traditions were effected for many centuries thereafter). The language is meant to be unshakeable, and its strict rules of rhetoric are meant not only to convey, but also to preserve, equally strict rules of logic, or, more really, equally permanent patterns of relationship. What was at stake in this formation of language in the service of permanence? Clearly, how things were said was intended to secure eternal preservation of what was said. Change affects the accidents and details. It cannot reshape enduring principles, and language will be used to effect their very endurance. What is said, moreover, is not to be subjected to pragmatic experimentation. The unstated but carefully considered principles shape reality and are not shaped and tested by and against reality. Use of pat phrases and syntactical clichés divorced from different thoughts to be said and different ways of thinking testifies to the prevailing notion of unstated, but secure and unchanging, reality behind and beneath the accidents of context and circumstance.

Clearly, so far as Middle Hebrew serves as a secular language, the Mishnah has transformed a common speech to sacred language and has done so through peculiar formalization of syntactical structures in particular. Yet we cannot point to anything intrinsically sacred even in those structures and patterns. For example, there is no use of the divine name, no tendency either to cite, let alone to model sentences after those of, sacred Scripture. Indeed, Scripture is treated with remarkable disinterest. The treatment of leprosy in Leviticus Chapters Thirteen and Fourteen follows an illogical thematic scheme. Negaim revises that theme and introduces the appropriate correction. Our Division is remarkably uninterested in Scriptural proofs for its propositions. Accordingly, what serves as the vehicle of sanctification is the imposition upon common speech of fixed, secular patterns of syntax, which functionally transform talk about common things into sacred language through the employment of certain stereotype patterns. What is regular is sacred. These patterns themselves on the surface, as I said, are routine and secular, yet in function accomplish the sanctification of language, its transformation into something other than, and different from, ordinary speech. We should expect distinctive word-choices, but I discern none. (By contrast, a story at b. Qiddushin 70a-b states that rabbis have their own language, different from that of ordinary folk. At no point does our division of the Mishnah contain an equivalent suggestion.) Who used the Mishnah's language? Clearly, people who memorized the Mishnah used it. To them was accorded significant status in the later schools. But that does not answer the question, Who first used this language and for what purpose? The answer by now is familiar. It was a group which proposed to create a document which would be transmitted by memory and therefore required formulation which would facilitate the mnemonic process.

Two facts have been established. First, the formalization of the Mishnaic thought-units is separate from the utilization of sound and other extrinsic characteristics of word-choice. It depends, rather, upon recurrent grammatical patterns independent of the choices of words set forth in strings. The listener or reader has to grasp relations of words, in a given sequence of sentences, quite separate from the substantive character of the words themselves.

Accordingly, second, the natural language of Middle Hebrew is not apt to be represented by the highly formal language of the Mishnah. The Mishnaic language constitutes something more than a random sequence of words using routinely to say things. It is meant as a highly formulaic way of expressing a particular set of distinctive conceptions. It is, therefore, erroneous to refer to Mishnaic-language; rather, we deal with the Mishnaic revision of the natural language of Middle Hebrew. And, it is clear, what the Mishnah does to revise that natural language is ultimately settled in the character of the grammar, inclusive of syntax, of the language. Middle Hebrew has a great many more grammatical sequences than does the Mishnaic Hebrew, and, it follows, Mishnaic Hebrew declares ungrammatical -- that is, refuses to make use of -- constructions which Middle Hebrew will regard as wholly grammatical and entirely acceptable.

The single striking trait of the formalization of the Mishnaic language therefore is that it depends upon grammar. And just as, by definition, "Grammar is autonomous and independent of meaning" (Chomsky, p. 17), so in the Mishnah, the formalization of thought into recurrent patterns is beneath the surface and independent of discrete meanings. Yet the Mishnah imposes its own discipline, therefore its own deeper level of unitary meaning, upon everything and anything which actually is said.

To summarize our discussion of Mishnaic rhetoric, let us now ask about the ecology of Mishnaic modes of speech (Haugen, pp. 337-7). What is its classification in relationship to other languages? A variety of Middle Hebrew, it is used in particular by people engaged in the memorization and transmission of teachings on behalf of which is claimed divine revelation. Accordingly, its users are religious specialists. What are the domains of use? So far as we know, the Mishnah's distinctive modes of speech are particular to the Mishnah. But this judgment must be qualified. Even in the Tosefta the same modes do not consistently occur and scarcely serve to characterize intermediate divisions. Accordingly, what is particular to the Mishnah is not the remarkably distinctive sentence-structures we have discerned, but recurrent use of such sentence-structures to give expression to sizable groups of cognitive units. That indeed is a limited domain of use. What concurrent languages are employed by the users of this mode of speech? Clearly, we may assume, Middle Hebrew in non-Mishnaic patterns was available to them. Whether in addition they spoke Aramaic or Greek is not equivalently clear, nor do we know that they spoke Middle Hebrew as a language of ordinary use. Accordingly, we do know the dialinguistical data necessary to answer this question.

Does the Mishnah yield evidence of dialect? The answer is clearly that it does not. On the contrary, the speech is decidedly uniform and unnuanced. To what degree has the Mishnaic variety of Middle Hebrew been standardized, unified and codified? Here the answer is clear. We have the highest degree of standardization.

What kind of institutional support stands behind the Mishnah? The answer is not wholly clear from the data we have examined. I am inclined to think that, if we take seriously the claim in behalf of the Mishnah that it is Oral Torah, then we have to assign to the Mishnah the claim of an extraordinary sort of Heavenly support for its variety of patterns of speech. But we must answer in secular, not mythic, terms. The Mishnah probably was supported through the activities of those who memorized the language and those who supported them, a wide circle of savants.

What are the attitudes of the users toward the language? It certainly is public and ritualistic, not a language of intimacy. Its use assuredly confers upon the user a defined status, leading to personal identification as a Tanna in the schools and and a rabbi outside of them. (But the evidence in behalf of these claims is not within the Mishnah itself.)

Finally, how does the Mishnaic variety of Hebrew relate to other languages? The answer is, of course, that it is not a language at all, but rather, a variety of a language, limited and formalized for special purposes. Its ecology will then share the profile of cultic languages in general, with the qualification that, if Middle Hebrew was widely used, it is a revision of a common language into a cultic language. Its relatedness to, and difference from, unpatterned Middle Hebrew serves to shape and express the ethos and world-view of a particular speech-community.

iii. Mnemonics and Meaning

In the absence of more than episodic evidence, we must speculate about the purpose of the editing of the Mishnah in final form solely by systematically extrapolating from the facts of its redaction insight into the purpose of its redaction. What we learn from the character of the literature about the circle that produced the literature, so far as that character speaks of those who created it, is nothing whatsoever. The people who made the Mishnah do not want us to know them, because, I should imagine, nothing about them was deemed important in the understanding of what they did. That is why they do not organize materials around given names of authorities, though as I said, some such constructions do survive. It is futile to ask whether the redactors were lawyers, philosophers, wonder-workers, teachers, government officials, preachers, soldiers, holy men, priests, anointed messiahs, or any of the other things people who produce a holy document such as this might have been. To ask whether they legislated for themselves or for all Israelites is equally hopeless, because, as we know, silent as they are on themselves, so reticent are they about those to whom they seek to speak.

Yet they do take certain things for granted. In order to make sense of what they do tell us, there are things which we have to know and which are not told to us by them. But from the perspective of form and rhetoric the catalogue hardly is a long one.

The Mishnah presupposes the existence of Scripture. It is not possible to make sense of the details of any tractate without knowledge of Scriptural laws. Yet what, in rhetoric and grammar, is it about, and in, Scripture that is presupposed? It is not, I have stressed, the style and language of Scripture. It is necessary to know certain facts of Scripture, e.g., that a corpse contaminates, that there is a dimension of the clean and the unclean. The knowledge even of facts of Scripture by themselves cannot, of course, suffice. The Mishnah has distinctive conceptions even of the meaning of simple facts, data of Scripture themselves. In the present context, what is important is that knowledge of Scripture's forms and style in no important way improves understanding of those of the Mishnah or even is relevant to interpreting them.

Yet there is a side to Scripture which, I think, is at the very bedrock of the Mishnah's linguistic character and explains the Mishnah's self-evident preoccupation with the interplay of theme and form. Scripture speaks of creation through words, and, we know, it is as much through how things are said as through what is said that the Mishnah proposes to effect its own creative purpose. The priestly notion of creation by means of speech is carried through in the Mishnah's most distinctive and ubiquitous attributive, X 'WMR, one says, just as at Genesis 1:3, 6, 9, 11, 14, 20, 24, 29, at each of he stages of creation, God says ('MR) something and it is. The supposition of the Mishnah that Scripture is known is, while not trivial, obvious.

There is a second, less blatant supposition. It is that the language of the Mishnah will be understood, its nuances appreciated, its points of stress and emphasis grasped. Our discussion of the cathectically neutral and indifferent style of the Mishnah, its failure to speak to some distinct audience in behalf of some defined speaker, does not obscure the simple fact that the Mishnah is not gibberish, but a corpus of formed and intensely meaningful statements, the form of which is meant to bear deep meaning. Accordingly, the gnomic sayings of the Mishnah, corresponding in their deep, universal grammar to the subterranean character of reality, permit the inference that the reality so described was to be grasped and understood by people of mind. Given the unarticulated points at which stress occurs, the level of grammar autonomous of discrete statements and concrete rulings, moreover, we must conclude that the framers of the Mishnah expected to be understood by remarkably keen ears and active minds. Conveying what is fundamental at the level of grammar autonomous of meaning, they manifested confidence that the listener will put many things together and draw the important conclusions for himself or herself. That means that the Mishnah assumes an active intellect, capable of perceiving inferred convention, and a vividly participating audience, capable of following what was said with intense concentration.

This demands, first, memorizing the message, second, perceiving the subtle and unarticulated message of the medium of syntax and, grammar. The hearer, third, is assumed to be capable of putting the two together into the still further insight that the cogent pattern exhibited by diverse statements preserves a substantive cogency among those diverse and delimited statements. Superficially-various rules, stated in sentences unlike one another on the surface and made up of unlike word-choices, in fact say a single thing in a single way. None of this is possible, it goes without saying, without anticipating that exegesis of the fixed text will be undertaken by the audience. The Mishnah demands commentary. It takes for granted that the audience is capable of exegesis and proposes to undertake the work. The Mishnah commands a sophisticated and engaged socio-intellectual context within the Israelite world. The Mishnah's lack of specificity on this point should not obscure its quite precise expectation: The thing it does not tell us which we have to know is that the Mishnah will be understood. The process of understanding, the character of the Mishnah's language testifies, is complex and difficult. The Mishnah is a document which compliments its audience.

Language serves the authorities of the Mishnah as an instrument of power, specifically, power to create reality. Wittgenstein (cited by Farb, p. 192) said, "The limits of my language mean the limits of my world." What are the limitations of the Mishnah's formalized modes of speech? What sort of reality is made possible within them and is constructed by them? To what degree, specifically, does Mishnaic language attain new possibilities for the containment and creation of reality precisely by its tendency to avoid explicit generalizations and its perpetual expression of precise but abstract relationships between things only in concrete terms? And, finally, we return to the central and inescapable question, For what purpose was the Mishnah made?

We begin, as we did above, with the gnomic character of the Mishnaic discourse. Clearly, the Mishnah claims to make wise and true statements, statements which, moreover, apply at any time and in any place. It follows, second, that the Mishnah proposes to describe how things truly are. And third, accordingly, the people who made the Mishnah did so in order to put together, in a single document and in encapsulated form, an account of the inner structure of reality, specifically, of that aspect of reality which, in their judgment, is susceptible of encapsulation in formally-patterned words. When, fourth, we recall the exceedingly limited repertoire of ways by which statements are made, we recognize that, to the authorities of the Mishnah, all of the diverse and changing things in the world can be reduced to a few simple, descriptive equations. These fifth, are to be expressed in particular by the inner and deep traits of the interrelationships of words, by persistent patterns of grammar and of syntax, rather than by superficial traits of sound and repetition of concrete thought. The principle is to be derived by the listener's reflection upon any set of diverse rules or statements, his contributed perception of what unites the whole, which will be left unsaid but everywhere deemed obvious.

Relying entirely on the traits of syntax and grammar which are before us, what can we say about the deepest convictions concerning reality characteristic of people who spoke in the ways we have considered? There is a deep sense of balance, of complementarity, of the appropriateness of opposites in the completion of a whole thought. Many times do we hear: if thus, then so, and if not thus, then not so. Mishnaic rhetoric demands, because the Mishnah's creators' sense of grammar requires, the completion of the positive by the negative, and of the negative by the positive. The contrastive complex predicate is testimony to the datum that order consists in completion and wholeness. So, too, the many balanced declarative sentences before us reveal the same inner conviction that in the completion of a pattern, in the working out of its single potentiality through a sequence of diverse actualities, lie that besought order and wholeness. The fact that it is the intermediate division which constitutes the formulary context of the Mishnah needs no further specification. Accidents do require specification and repetition. The Mishnah is scarcely satisfied to give a single instance of a rule, from which we may generalize. It strongly prefers to give us three or six or nine instances, on the basis of which we may then conclude that there is, indeed, an underlying rule. The singleton-case is not the rule solely for itself, nor, all by itself, for all things.

I do not perceive an equivalent meaning in the duplicated subject. When, however, we come to apocopation -- beside the sequentially balanced sentence, the Mishnah's other remarkable formulary structure -- we once more perceive something from the external expression about the mind, the inner structure of which is subject to articulation. What do we have in apocopation? It is, first of all, a powerful sense of superficial incompleteness and disorder. Apocopated sentences are composed of disjoined phrases. The subject of such sentences generally is made up of two or more such phrases, each of them introducing its own actor and acted-upon, its subject and predicate. What unites the several clauses and imposes meaning upon all of them is the ultimate predicate. This, by itself, cannot always be asked to refer to any single one of the phrases of the subject. But it encompasses the result of all of them, all together. It is, therefore, a construction the meaning of which depends upon a context which is inferred from, but not made explicit by, its constituents. In a profound sense, the apocopated sentence, which we found so distinctive to the Mishnah, expresses that deep sense of a wholeness beneath discrete parts which Mishnaic language presupposes.

For it is the mind of the hearer which makes sense of the phrases and clauses of the subject and perceives the relationship, endowing whole meaning upon the clauses of the subject, required by the predicate. The mind of the hearer is central in the process by which apocopation attains meaning. The capacity for perceiving the rational and orderly sense of things exhibited by that mind is the unstated necessity of apocopation. That, as we have seen in the preceding discussion, is characteristic of Mishnaic modes of expression, therefore also of perception. Hearing discrete rules, applicable to cases related in theme and form, but not in detail and concrete actualities, the hearer puts together two things. First is the repetition of grammatical usages. Second is the repetition of the same principle, the presence of which is implied by the repetition of syntactical patterns in diverse cases. These two, stable principle and disciplined grammar autonomous of meaning, are never stated explicitly but invariably present implicitly.

So there are these two striking traits of mind reflected within Mishnaic rhetoric: first, the perception of order and balance, second, the perception of the mind's centrality in the construction of order and balance, the imposition of wholeness upon discrete cases, in the case of the routine declarative sentence, and upon discrete phrases, in the case of the apocopated one. Both order and balance are contained from within and are imposed from without. The relationships revealed by deep grammatical consistencies internal to a sentence and the implicit regularities revealed by the congruence and cogency of specified cases rarely are stated but always are to be discerned. Accordingly, the one thing which the Mishnah invariably does not make explicit but which always is necessary to know is, I stress, the presence of the active intellect, the participant who is the hearer. It is the hearer who ultimately makes sense of, perceives the sense in, the Mishnah. Once more we are impressed by the Mishnah's expectation of high sophistication and profound sensitivity to order and to form on the part of its impalpable audience.

In this sense the Mishnah serves both as a book of laws and as a book for learners, a law-code and a school-book. But it is in this sense alone.

If our Division of the Mishnah is a law-code, it is remarkably reticent about punishments for infractions of its rules. It rarely says what one must do, or must not do, if he or she becomes unclean, and hardly even alludes to punishments or rewards consequent upon disobedience or obedience to its laws. "Clean" and "unclean" rhetorically are the end of the story and generate little beyond themselves.

If our Division serves as a school-book, it never informs us about its institutional setting, speaks of its teachers, sets clearcut perceptible educational goals for its students, and, above all, attempts to stand in relationship to some larger curriculum or educational and social structure. Its lack of context and unselfconsciousness framework of discourse hardly support the view that, in a this-worldly and ordinary sense, we have in our hands a major division of a law-code or of a school-book.

Nor is the Mishnah a corpus of traditions which lay claim to authority or to meaning by virtue of the authorities cited therein. That is why the name of an authority rarely serves as a redactional fulcrum. As I have stressed, the tense-structure is ahistorical and anti-historical. Sequences of actions generally are stated in the descriptive present tense. Rules attain authority not because of who says them, but because (it would seem) no specific party at a specific time stands behind them. The reason, I think that shortly after the promulgation of the Mishnah, the Mishnah gained for itself the place in the revealed Torah of Moses at Sinai, testifies against its capacity to serve as an essentially historical statement of who said what, when, and for which purpose. The Mishnah, as I have emphasized, is descriptive of how things are. It is indifferent to who has said so, uninterested in the cumulative past behind what it has to say. These are not the traits of a corpus of "traditions." I am inclined to think that law-code, school-book, and corpus of traditions all are not quite to the point of the accurate characterization of the Mishnah.

Yet, if not quite to the point, all nonetheless preserve a measure of proximate relevance to the definition of the Mishnah. The Mishnah does contain descriptive laws. These laws require the active participation of the mind of the hearer, thus are meant to be learned, not merely obeyed, and self-evidently are so shaped as to impart lessons, not merely rules to be kept. The task of the hearer is not solely or primarily to obey, though I think obedience is taken for granted, but to participate in the process of discovering principles and uncovering patterns of meaning. The very form of Mishnaic rhetoric, its formalization and the function of that form testify to the role of the learner and hearer, that is, the student, in the process of definitive and indicative description, not communication, of what is and of what is real. Self-evidently, the Mishnah's citation of authorities makes explicit the claim that some men, now dead, have made their contribution, therefore have given shape and substance to tradition, that which is shaped by one and handed onward by another. So the Mishnah indeed is, and therefore is meant as, a law-code, a school-book, and a corpus of tradition. It follows that the purpose for which the Mishnah was edited into final form was to create such a multi-purpose document, a tripartite goal attained in a single corpus of formed and formal sayings. And yet, it is obvious, the Mishnah is something other than these three things in one. It transcends the three and accomplishes more than the triple goals which on the surface form the constitutive components of its purpose.

To describe that transcendent purpose, we return to Wittgenstein's saying. "The limits of my language mean the limits of my world." The Mishnah's formulaic rhetoric on the one side imposes limits, boundaries, upon the world. What fits into that rhetoric, can be said by it, constitutes world, world given shape and boundary by the Mishnah. The Mishnah implicitly maintains, therefore, that a wide range of things fall within the territory mapped out by a limited number of linguistic conventions, grammatical sentences. What is grammatical can be said and therefore constitutes part of the reality created by Mishnaic word. What cannot be contained within the grammar of the sentence cannot be said and therefore falls outside of the realm of Mishnaic reality. Mishnaic reality consists in those things which can attain order, balance, and principle. Chaos then lies without. Yet, if we may extrapolate from the capacity of the impoverished repertoire of grammar to serve for all sorts of things, for the eleven topics of our division, for example, then we must concede that all things can be said by formal revision. Everything can be reformed, reduced to the order and balance and exquisite sense for the just match characteristic of the Mishnaic pericope. Anything of which we wish to speak is susceptible of the ordering and patterning of Mishnaic grammar and syntax. That is a fact which is implicit throughout our division. Accordingly, the territory mapped out by Mishnaic language encompasses the whole of the pertinent world under discussion. There are no thematic limitations of Mishnaic formalized speech.

Yet reality, the world of clean and unclean in the present context, is forced to surpass itself, to strive for a higher level of order and meaning through its submission to Mishnaic formalization. Implicit in the rhetoric of our document is the notion, now alluded to many times, of deep regularities which in principle unite cases, just as regularities in rhetoric unite cases. What is abstract need not be spelled out and instantiated endlessly because it already is spelled out through recurrent, implicit relationships among words, among cases. In this context we recall Green's statement, "If the performance of rituals within the Temple exposes the lines of God's revealed reality, then thinking ... about these rituals outside the Temple, even without the possibility of performing all of them, has the same result. The Mishnaic rabbis express their primary cognitive statements, their judgments upon large matters, through ... law, not through myth or theology, neither of which is articulated at all. Early Rabbinism took ritual beyond the realm of practice and transformed it into the object of speculation and the substance of thought. Study, learning, and exposition became ... the basic Rabbinic activity ..." Restating this view in terms of Mishnaic grammatical rhetoric, we may say that the thinking about matters of detail within a particular pattern of cognitive constructions treats speculation and thought as themselves capable of informing and shaping being, not merely expressing its external traits: Language becomes ontology.

Language in the Mishnah replaces cult, formalism of one kind takes the place of formalism of another. The claim that infinitely careful and patterned doing of a particular sort of deeds is ex opere operato an expression of the sacred has its counterpart in the implicit character of the Mishnah's language. Its rhetoric is formed with infinite care, according to a finite pattern for speech, about doing deeds for a particular sort. Language now conforms to cult then. The formal cult, once performed in perfect silence, now is given its counterpart in formal speech. Where once men said nothing, but through gesture and movement, in other circumstances quite secular, performed holy deed, now they do nothing, but through equally patterned revision of secular words about secular things perform holy speech. In the cult it is the very context which makes an intrinsically neutral, therefore secular, act into a holy one. Doing the thing right, with precision and studied care, makes the doing holy. Slaughtering an animal, collecting its blood and butchering it, burning incense and pouring wine -- these by themselves are things which can be and are done in the home as much as in the cult. But in the cult they are characterized by formality and precision. In the Mishnah, by contrast, there is no spatial context to sanctify the secular act of saying things. The context left, once cult is gone, is solely the cultic mode of formalism, the ritualization of speech, that most neutral and commonplace action. The Mishnah transforms speech into ritual and so creates the surrogate of ritual deed. That which was not present in cult, speech, is all that is present now that the silent cult is gone. And, it follows, it is by the formalization of speech, its limitation to a few patterns, and its perfection through the creation of patterns of relationships in particular, that the old nexus of Heaven and earth, the cult, now is to be replicated in the new and complementary nexus, cultic speech about all things.

What the limitation of Mishnaic language to a few implicit relational realities accomplished, therefore, is the reduction of the world to the limits of language. In ritual-grammar the world therein contained and expressed attains formalization among, and simplification by, the unstated but remarkably few principles contained within, and stated by, the multitudinous cases which correspond to the world. Mishnaic language makes possible the formalization of the whole of the everyday and workaday world. It accomplishes the transformation of all things in accord with that sense for perfect form and unfailing regularity which once were distinctive to the operation of the cult. Mishnaic language explores the possibility of containing and creating a new realm of reality, one which avoids abstractions and expresses all things only through the precision of grammatical patterns, that is, the reality of abstract relationships alone.

Have we come closer to a perception of the purpose for which, according to the internal testimony of our order, the Mishnah was created? In a concrete sense, of course, we have not. Mishnaic rhetoric says nothing explicit about the purpose of the rhetoric. In the simplest sense, as we noted, the proximate purpose of formalization was to facilitate the mnemonic process. Yet it is to beg the question to say that the purpose of facilitating memorization is to help people remember things. The authors of the Mishnah wants their book to be memorized for a reason. The reason transcends the process, pointing, rather, to its purpose. Nor do we stand closer to the inner intentions of the Mishnah's authorities when we raise the polemical purpose of memorization. This was to act out the claim that there are two components of "the one whole Torah which Moses, our rabbi, received from God at Sinai," one transmitted in writing, the other handed on by tradition, in oral form only. True, the claim for the Mishnah, laid down in Abot, the Mishnah's first and most compelling apologetic, is that the authority of the Mishnah rests upon its status as received tradition of God. It follows that tradition handed on through memory is valid specifically because, while self-evidently not part of the written Torah, which all Israel has in hand, it is essential to the whole Torah. Its mode of tradition through memory verifies and authenticates its authority as tradition begun by God, despite its absence from the written part of Torah. Both these things -- the facilitation of memorization, the authentication of the document through its external form -- while correct also are post facto. They testify to the result of Mishnaic rhetoric for both educational-tradental and polemical-apologetic purposes. Once we memorize, we accomplish much. But why, to begin with, commit these gnomic sayings to such language as facilitates their memorization?

In a world such as the Mishnah's, in which writing is routine, memorization is special. What happens when we know something by heart which does not happen when we must read it or look for it in a scroll or a book? It is that when we walk in the street and when we sit at home, when we sleep and when we awake, we carry with us, in our everyday perceptions, that memorized gnomic saying. The process of formulation through formalization and the coequal process of memorizing patterned cases to sustain the perception of the underlying principle, uniting the cases just as the pattern unites their language, extend the limits of language to the outer boundaries of experience, the accidents of everyday life itself. Gnomic sayings are routine in all cultures. But the reduction of all truth particularly to gnomic sayings is not.

To impose upon those sayings an underlying and single structure of grammar corresponding to the inner structure of reality is to transform the structure of language into a statement of ontology. Once our minds are trained to perceive principle among cases and pattern within grammatical relationships, we further discern in the concrete events of daily life both principle and underlying autonomous pattern. The form of the Mishnah is meant to correspond to the formalization perceived within, not merely imposed upon, the conduct of concrete affairs, principally, the meaning and character of concrete happenings among things, in the workaday life of people. The matter obviously is not solely ethical, but the ethical component is self-evident. It also has to do with the natural world and the things which break its routine, of which our Division speaks so fully and in such exquisite detail. Here all things are a matter of relationship, circumstance, fixed and recurrent interplay. If X, then Y, if not X, then not Y -- that is the datum by which minds are shaped.

The way to shape and educate minds is to impart into the ear, thence into the mind, perpetual awareness that what happens recurs, and what recurs is pattern and order, and, through them, wholeness. How better than to fill the mind with formalized sentences, generative both of meaning for themselves and of significance beyond themselves, in which meaning rests upon the perception of relationship? Pattern is to be discovered in alertness, in the multiplicity of events and happenings, none of which states or articulates pattern. Mind, trained to memorize through what is implicit and beneath the surface, is to be accustomed and taught in such a way as to discern pattern. Order is because order is discovered, first in language, then in life. As the cult in all its precise and obsessive attention to fixed detail effected the perception that from the orderly center flowed lines of meaning to the periphery, so the very language of the Mishnah, in the particular traits which I have specified, also in its precise and obsessive concentration on innate and fixed relationship, effects the perception of order deep within the disorderly world of language, nature, and man.

So to conclude: There is a perfect correspondence between what the Mishnah proposes to say and the way in which it says it. An essential part of the ethos of Mishnaic culture is its formal and formulaic sentence, the means by which it makes its cognitive statements and so expresses its world-view. Not only does ethos correspond to world-view, but world-view is expressed in style as much as in substance. In the case of Mishnaic form, the ethos and world-view come together in the very elements of grammatical formalization, which, never made articulate, express the permanence and paramount character of relationship, the revelatory relativity of context and circumstance. Life attains form in structure. It is structure which is most vivid in life. The medium for the expression of the world-view is the ethos. But for the Mishnah, ethos neither appeals to, nor, so far as I can see, expresses, emotion. Just as there is no room for nuance in general in the severe and balanced sentences of the Mishnah, so there is no place for the nuance of emotion of commitment in general. How so? The rhetoric of our document makes no appeal to emotion or to obedience, describing, not invoking, the compelling and ineluctable grounds for assent. This claim that things are such and so, relate in such and such a way, without regard or appeal to how we want them to be, is unyielding. Law is law, despite the accidents of workaday life, and facts are facts. The bearer of facts, the maker of law, is the relationship, the pattern by which diverse things are set into juxtaposition with one another, whether subject and predicate, or dead creeping thing and loaf of Heave-offering. What is definitive is not the thing but the context and the circumstance, the time, the condition, the intention of the actor. In all, all things are relative to all things.

The bridge from ethos to world-view is the form and character of the sentence which transforms the one into the other. The declarative sentence through patterned language takes attitude and turns it into cognition. Mishnaic "religion" not only speaks of values. Its mode of speech is testimony to its highest and most enduring, distinctive value. This language does not speak of sacred symbols but of pots and pans, of menstruation and dead creeping things, of ordinary water which, because of the circumstance of its collection and location, possesses extraordinary power, of the commonplace corpse and the ubiquitous diseased person, of genitalia and excrement, toilet-seats and the flux of penises, of stems of pomegranates and stalks of leeks, of rain and earth and clay ovens, wood, metal, glass, and hide. This language is filled with words for neutral things of humble existence. It does not speak of holy things and is not symbolic in its substance. In the Mishnah, Holy Things are merely animals a farmer has designated, in his intention, as holy. The language of the Mishnah speaks of ordinary things, of workaday things which everyone must have known. But because of the peculiar and particular way in which it is formed and formalized, this same language not only adheres to an aesthetic theory but expresses a deeply-embedded ontology and methodology of the sacred, specifically of the sacred within the secular, and of the capacity for regulation, therefore for sanctification, within the ordinary.

World-view and ethos are synthesized in language. The synthesis is expressed in grammatical and syntactical regularities. What is woven into some sort of ordered whole is not a cluster of sacred symbols. The religious system is not discerned within symbols at all. Knowledge of the conditions of life is imparted principally through the description of the commonplace facts of life, which symbolize, stand for, nothing beyond themselves and their consequences for the clean and the unclean. That description is effected through the construction of units of meaning, intermediate divisions composed of cognitive elements. The whole is balanced, explicit in detail, but reticent about the whole, balanced in detail but dumb about the character of the balance. What is not said is what is eloquent and compelling as much as what is said. Accordingly, that simple and fundamental congruence between ethos and world-view is to begin with, for the Mishnah, the very language by which the one is given cognitive expression in the other. The medium of patterned speech conveys the meaning of what is said.

REFERENCES AND ABBREVIATIONS

Ah.   =   'Ahilot [= Tosefta's title for M. 'Ohalot.]
Albeck   =   H. Albeck, Seder tohorot (Jerusalem and Tel Aviv, 1958).
Ar.   =   ^CArakhin
A.Z.   =   ^CAbodah Zarah
B.   =   Babli, Babylonian Talmud
B.B.   =   Baba' Batra'
B.M.   =   Baba' Mesi^Ca'
B.Q.   =   Baba' Qamma'
Ber.   =   Berakhot
Bes.   =   Besah
Bik.   =   Bikkurim
Chomsky, Language   =   Noam Chomsky, Language and Mind (N.Y., 1972).
Chomsky, Reflections   =   Noam Chomsky, Reflections on Language (N.Y., 1975).
Chomsky, Structures   =   Noam Chomsky, Syntactic Structures (The Hague, 1957).
Dan.   =   Daniel
Dem.   =   Demai
Deut.   =   Deuteronomy
Douglas   =   Mary   Douglas,   Natural   Symbols.   Explorations   in
                              Cosmology (N.Y., 1970. Used: Vintage Books edition,
                              1973).
Ed.   =   ^CEduyyot
Erub.   =   ^CErubin
Epstein, Nussah   =   See Nussah.
Epstein, Tan.   =   See Tan.
Farb, Word Play   =   Peter Farb, Word Play. What Happens When People Talk
                              (N.Y., 1974. Used: Bantam edition, N.Y., 1975).
Fishman   =   Joshua A. Fishman, The Sociology of Language. An
                              Interdisciplinary Social Science Approach to Language in
                              Society (Rosley, 1972).
Fitzmyer   =   Joseph A. Fitzmyer, "The Languages of Palestine in the
                              First Century A.D.," Catholic Biblical Quarterly 32, 1970,
                              pp. 501-531.
Geertz, Ethos   =   Clifford Geertz, "Ethos, World-View and the Analysis of
                              Sacred Symbols," The Antioch Review 17, 4, 1957, pp.
                              421-437.
Geertz, Religion   =   Clifford   Geertz,   "Religion   as   a   Cultural   System,"
                              Anthropological Approaches to the Study of Religion,
                              Edited by Michael Banton (London, 1966), pp. 1-46.

Git.	=	Gittin.
Green, Bibliography	=	William Scott Green, "What's in a Name? The Problematic of Rabbinic 'Biography'," in Approaches to Ancient Judaism, ed. by William Scott Green (Missoula, 1977).
Hag.	=	Hagigah
Hal.	=	Hallah
Harmon	=	On Noam Chomsky: Critical Essays. Edited by Gilbert Harmon (N.Y., 1974).
Haugen	=	Einar Haugen, The Ecology of Language (Stanford, 1972).
Hor.	=	Horayot
Hul.	=	Hullin
Jastrow	=	Marcus Jastrow, A Dictionary of the Targumim, etc. (Reprint N.Y., 1950).
Kel.	=	Kelim
Ker.	=	Keritot
Kil.	=	Kilayim
Lane	=	Introduction to Structuralism. Edited and Introduced by Michael Lane (N.Y., 1979). Consulted: R. Barthes, "Historical Discourse," pp. 145-155; M. Gaboriau, "Structural Anthropology and History," pp. 156-169; E. Leach, "The Legitimacy of Solomon," pp. 248-292.
Lev.	=	Leviticus
Lévy-Bruhl	=	Lucien Lévy-Bruhl, How Natives Think (London, 1926).
Lieberman, Publication	=	Saul Lieberman, "The Publication of the Mishnah," Hellenism in Jewish Palestine (N.Y., 1950), pp. 83-99.
M.	=	Mishnah
Ma.	=	Ma^{C}aserot
Mak.	=	Makkot
Makh.	=	Makhshirin
Me.	=	Me^{C}ilah
Meg.	=	Megillah
Melamed	=	E.Z. Melamed, Hayyahas sheben midrashé halakhah lammishnah velattosefta (Jerusalem, 1967).
Mellinkoff	=	David Mellinkoff, The Language of the Law (Boston, 1963).
Men.	=	Menahot
Miq.	=	Miqvaot
M.Q.	=	Mo^{C}ed Qatan
M.S.	=	Ma^{C}aser Sheni
MSM	=	The Modern Study of the Mishnah, edited by Jacob Neusner (Leiden, 1973).
Naz.	=	Nazir

Ned.	=	Nedarim
Neg.	=	Nega^{C}im
Nid.	=	Niddah
Num.	=	Numbers
Oh.	=	'Ohalot
Or.	=	^{C}Orlah
Par.	=	Parah
Pes.	=	Pesahim
Qid.	=	Qiddushin
R.H.	=	Rosh Hashshanah
Saldarini	=	Anthony J. Saldarini, review, History of the Mishnaic Law of Purities I-III, Journal of Biblical Literature 95, 1, 1976, pp. 149-151.
San.	=	Sanhedrin
Shab.	=	Shabbat
Shabu.	=	Shabu^{C}ot
Sheb.	=	Shebi^{C}it
Sheq.	=	Sheqalim
Sot.	=	Sotah
Spiro	=	Melford E. Spiro, "Religion: Problems of Definition and Explanation," in Anthropological Approaches to the Study of Religion. Edited by Michael Banton (London, 1966), pp. 85-126.
Stemberger	=	Günter Stemberger, "La recherche rabbinique depuis Strack," translated into French by R. Breckle. Revue d'histoire et de philosophie religieuses, 55, 4, 1975, pp. 543-574.
Strack	=	Hermann L. Strack, Introduction to the Talmud and Midrash (Philadelphia, 1931. Used: Harper Torchbook edition, N.Y., 1965).
Suk.	=	Sukkah
T.	=	Tosefta
Ta.	=	Ta^{C}anit
Tem.	=	Temurah
Ter.	=	Terumot
Toh.	=	Tohorot
TR	=	See Lieberman, TR.
T.Y.	=	Tebul Yom
Uqs.	=	^{C}Uqsin
Y.	=	Yerushalmi. Palestinian Talmud.
Y.T.	=	Yom Tob

Yad.	=	Yadayim
Yeb.	=	Yebamot
Zab.	=	Zabim
Zeb.	=	Zebahim

'MR
123
'P
11, 14, 16, 21, 22, 25, 27, 28, 44, 45,
50-54, 80, 81, 93, 108, 117, 121, 124
'WMR
111, 114, 116, 123
Apocopation
32, 33, 37, 38, 40-50, 52, 54, 56, 57,
67, 71-74, 89, 90, 94, 98-100,
102-105, 107, 114, 125
^CAqiba
14, 17, 27, 75, 76
Aramaic
5, 121
Chomsky, Noam
121, 133, 134
Declarative sentences
1, 34, 36-57, 59-61, 67, 70-81, 83, 86,
87, 89, 90, 94, 98-108, 111, 124
Farb, Peter
114, 117, 124, 133
Fishman, Joshua
133
Formulary trait
30, 39-42, 45, 47-51, 53, 55, 58, 61,
100, 105, 108, 31, 32, 35-37, 39, 40,
48, 53, 55, 57, 60, 70-72, 86, 109, 112
Galilee
2
Geertz, Clifford
133
Gnomic sayings
123, 129
God
1, 123, 127, 129
Grammar
113, 114, 117, 121, 123-25, 127-29
Green, William S.
115, 127, 134
He-who
19, 32, 34, 38, 40, 42, 43, 45-48,
51-54, 71, 72, 75, 77-80, 82, 84, 85,
89-94, 96-98, 100, 102-108, 114, 117,
118
Hebrew
1, 5, 69, 113, 120-22
Hillel
6, 9, 10, 15, 22, 23, 25-27, 75
If..., then...
6
Intermediate divisions
29, 31, 35, 36, 53, 55, 57, 59, 60, 62,
67, 69, 70, 72, 99, 100, 102, 104, 109,
111, 121, 131
Israel
1, 115, 129

Judaism
1, 8, 134
Language
1, 5-7, 10, 30, 31, 44, 69, 70, 107,
111-14, 116-18, 120-25, 127-31, 133,
134
Lieberman, Saul
27, 28, 112, 134, 135
MRBH
9
Ma^Caseh
9, 37, 43, 51, 56, 73, 81
Ma^Casim
119
Mellinkoff, David
111, 134
Meter
10, 14-16, 25
Mishnah
1-3, 5-7, 10, 27-30, 62, 67, 69, 70,
103, 108, 109, 111-31, 134
Mnemonics
1-3, 5, 7, 111, 122
Negative
12, 16, 18, 21, 25, 60, 124
Number
14, 16, 23, 25, 32, 36, 43, 58, 62, 99,
127
Oral
1, 8, 10, 27, 112, 122, 129
Pattern
2, 5-7, 9, 17, 18, 21, 25, 26, 30-40,
42, 43, 45-49, 52, 53, 55-58, 60, 61,
66, 67, 70, 71, 75, 76, 78, 79, 83, 86,
99-108, 111, 114, 115, 117, 118, 123,
124, 128-30
Patterns
1, 5-7, 9, 10, 15, 25, 26, 30, 31, 34,
37, 39, 41, 55, 56, 67, 69, 70, 72, 99,
103, 105-109, 111, 113-15, 117-22,
124-26, 128
Plato
2
Predicate
9, 10, 32, 34, 37-39, 45, 52, 54, 69-73,
83, 86, 88, 89, 94, 101, 102, 104-108,
124, 125, 130
Publication
27, 28, 134
Published
27, 112
Redaction
3, 10, 29, 31, 34, 35, 47, 53, 60, 69,
70, 100, 102, 103, 107, 109, 113, 122
Redactor
35, 49, 53, 60

BROWN JUDAIC STUDIES SERIES

Continued from back cover